The Humanist Tradition in the West

Alan Bullock
The Humanist Tradition in the West

with 148 illustrations, 27 in color

W.W. Norton & Company
New York   London

Frontispiece: The Parthenon

© Copyright 1985 Alan Bullock

First American Edition 1985

Published simultaneously in Canada by Penguin Books
Canada Ltd, 2801 John Street, Markham, Ontario L3R 1B4.

The text of this book is composed in Bembo.
Printed in Great Britain by Balding +
Mansell Limited, Wisbech, Cambs.
Bound in Great Britain

Library of Congress Cataloging in Publication Data

Bullock, Alan, 1914 –
The humanist tradition in the West.
"These lectures were delivered at the University Club,
New York, under the auspices of the Aspen Institute for
Humanistic Studies, in January–February 1984" – Pref.
Contents: The Renaissance – The Enlightenment –
The nineteenth century, rival versions – [etc.]
1. Humanism – History – Addresses, essays, lectures.
I. Title.
B821.B78 1985   144   85-4813

ISBN 0-393-02237-4

W. W. Norton & Company, Inc., 500 Fifth Avenue, New York,
N.Y. 10110.

W. W. Norton & Company Ltd, 37 Great Russell Street,
London WC1B 3NU

1 2 3 4 5 6 7 8 9 0

Contents

Preface

These lectures were delivered in College Hall at the University Club, New York, under the auspices of the Aspen Institute for Humanistic Studies, in January–February 1984.

They were an expression of gratitude to the Aspen Institute and its President, J. E. Slater, for the many benefits as well as pleasures which my wife and I have derived from our association with it. The lectures were named after the late Jessie K. Emmett, with whom we worked in the Aspen Institute and for whom we felt both affection and admiration as a woman whose attitude to life – and whose courage in the face of death – seemed to express some of the finest qualities of the humanist tradition.

I wish to express my gratitude to Eva Popper for organizing the lectures on behalf of the Aspen Institute; to the Giles W. and Elise G. Mead Foundation for a grant to cover the expenses involved, and to Raphael Bernstein who has generously made it possible to include 16 pages of colour in the illustrations. I have been particularly fortunate in my publishers, Tom Wallace of W. W. Norton, whose idea it was to turn the lectures into a book, and Stanley Baron who has acted as editor and made available the resources of Thames and Hudson in finding illustrations.

A seminar organized by the Aspen Institute at the Baca Grande ranch, Crestone, Colorado, under the chairmanship of Colin Williams, provided comments and criticisms from which I have been able to profit in revising the text. I have taken advantage of publication to restore a number of passages which had to be omitted in order to keep each lecture within the compass of an hour's delivery. The material restored to the fourth lecture has made it disproportionately long, and I have therefore divided it between chapters 4 and 5 of the book. The book, however, retains the form of lectures and is substantially the same as the text from which I spoke in New York.

In the production of the final text and illustrations, I have received invaluable help from Mrs Pamela Thomas and Miss Suzanne Bosman.

My greatest debt, as always, is to my wife, who has shared the experiences and enthusiasms which have formed my view of the humanist tradition.

St Catherine's College,
Oxford   *1 September, 1984*

7

Introduction

I first became interested in the meaning of the words humanist and humanism when I became associated with the Aspen Institute for Humanistic Studies at the beginning of the 1970s. The Aspen Institute, like the Aspen Musical Festival, has its origins in the bicentennial celebrations of Goethe's birth in 1949 organized by Walter Paepcke, Robert Hutchins and G. A. Borgese of the University of Chicago, in what was then a ghost town left behind by the collapse of silver mining, 8,000 feet up in the Colorado Rockies. Among the speakers at the celebration[1] were Albert Schweitzer and the Spanish philosopher and social critic, Ortega y Gasset. The latter, who in 1948 had founded an *Instituto de Humanidades* in Madrid, of which he was Rector, proposed to Walter Paepcke that the Goethe celebrations should be followed by the creation of an Institute for Humanistic Studies in Aspen, and although the Institute took on a very different character from that suggested by Ortega, it retained the name he suggested and something of his original purpose.

I had spent my life in Oxford where humanistic studies have deep roots going back at least to Erasmus, Colet and More, and the New Learning of the Renaissance. Perhaps because of that, their meaning was taken for granted and it was not until I was in my late fifties and had become Vice Chancellor of Oxford that I sat down in the library of the Aspen Institute in the Rockies and asked myself what there was in common between the humanistic studies in which I had been educated and the sort of discussions organized by the Aspen Institute on the social and moral issues underlying the policy choices to be made in regard to justice, education, the revolution in communications, the environment, energy, arms control, and any other of the problems set for societies as different as the U.S.A., Japan and Britain by the impact of change.

I shall come back to this initial question in my final lecture, but in a search for an answer I came to see the problem I had posed in a much wider context. I found that humanism, humanist, humanistic and the humanities are words that no one has ever succeeded in defining to anyone else's satisfaction, protean words which mean very different things to different people and leave lexicographers and encyclopaedists with a feeling of exasperation and frustration.

Intrigued by the problem, over the past ten years I have continued to read anything I could find to which it seemed the word humanist could be applied, from Plato's Dialogues and the debate amongst historians about the Renaissance, to Locke, Goethe, John Stuart Mill, William James, Max Weber, Freud and Thomas Mann. These lectures retrace the route I followed and present a progress report on what I have found.

As a working hypothesis, I have taken humanism to be, not a school of thought or a philosophical doctrine, but a broad tendency, a dimension of thought and belief, a continuing debate within which at any one time there will be found very different – at times opposed – views, held together not by a unified structure but by certain shared assumptions and a preoccupation with certain characteristic problems and topics, which change from one period to the next. The best word I can find to describe it is the humanist tradition.

Whether I can convince you that I am justified in speaking of such a tradition is a question that can only be answered when I have completed my lectures. One obvious element would be the value attached to classical antiquity from Petrarch to Goethe and Matthew Arnold, and the common experience of a classical education. But the sense in which I use the term is not that of the conscious handing on of an unchanging belief or practice. It is rather the recognition, often retrospective, of a kinship of ideas and assumptions, such as Italian humanists recognized in Petrarch; the eighteenth-century *philosophes* in Locke; Mill in Bentham and Coleridge; Thomas Mann in Goethe; and William James in Montaigne. Those who educated young men and women of my generation in the humanities between the Wars believed that they were initiating us into such a tradition, and this belief strongly influenced their lives as it had those of many of the scholars and writers who were refugees from Nazism, and as it has shaped my own.

The principal names to include in the tradition choose themselves. For the earlier period I have little more to do than add Alberti, Erasmus, Voltaire, Diderot to those I have already mentioned. But the inclusion or exclusion of others, especially as one comes closer to our own time, represents a personal choice. This would be true of anyone else's version, but lecturing in New York I particularly regret having too little knowledge of the history of ideas in the United States to do justice to the American contribution; with few exceptions my material is drawn from European sources.

One last point, and I have finished with my introduction. I take the words humanism and humanistic to apply as much to women as to men. But the tradition I am examining is an historical one, and up to the twentieth century the common usage was to use the word Man as the equivalent of the human species. Whenever I speak in my own person I shall speak of men and women, or of the human race; but when such phrases as the Fall of Man or the Dignity of Man occur in an historical context, which I am either quoting or paraphrasing, I shall leave the original as it stands.

Chapter One

The Renaissance

I

The first and most obvious clue to follow in my inquiry was to look at the history of the words humanism, humanistic and the humanities. That takes one straight back to the world of antiquity. But the Latin word *humanitas* from which our words derive was itself a Roman version of an older Greek idea. The ancient Greeks, besides inventing philosophy, history and drama (for which we still use the Greek words), also invented education, at least in the Western world. Under the name *paideia* (derived from the Greek word *pais, paides*, meaning a boy or child, which also gives us pediatrics, pedagogy, and for that matter pederasty), it was already old when it was systematized in Athens in the fifth and fourth centuries BC. It had four characteristics.

It offered a unified and systematic account of human knowledge in the seven liberal arts which was eventually, centuries later in the Middle Ages, to set the original pattern of university education – the liberal arts of grammar, rhetoric, logic or dialectics (the *trivium*) and arithmetic, geometry, astronomy and harmony (the *quadrivium*).

It provided a technique of teaching and disputation in a world without books, based upon mastery of language, intellectual precision and dialectical skill.

It made one of the great assumptions of Western civilization – that it is possible to mould the development of the human personality by education.

Finally, in the concept of the human excellence it sought to develop, it included the qualities of persuasion and leadership needed to play an active role in public affairs – a role which the Greeks regarded as essential to a man's humanity.

Greece and its small city-states were conquered and swallowed up in the empires of Macedon and Rome, but the Greek language and Greek education spread and enjoyed a unique prestige from the Atlantic to the borders of China. The Greeks' *paideia* was taken over by the Romans and given classical form by Cicero and Quintilian in their treatises on education, the titles of which in both cases were linked to oratory.[2]

In the Roman as in the Greek world, with no printed books, newspapers or other media of communication, public affairs were conducted face to face in assemblies and law courts, and mastery of the arts of the orator was the key to influence and power. But this meant not

2–10 Petrarch, Alberti, Lorenzo de Medici, Michelangelo, Erasmus, Machiavelli, Thomas More, Montaigne, Marguerite of Navarre

11

only the ability to speak well – and it was the power of speech which the Romans saw as distinguishing man from the other animals – but the mental power to grasp and present or criticize an argument, calling for a well-rounded education in the liberal arts. The Greek phrase for this was *enkyklia paedeia* (the origin of our word Encyclopaedia), for which Cicero found an equivalent in the Latin word *humanitas*, following the Greek view that this was the way to develop those qualities which are uniquely human and humane.

This Graeco-Roman tradition exercised an extraordinary influence on Western education until the end of the nineteenth century. It certainly shaped my own, in the 1930s in the most prestigious of Oxford courses, known as 'Greats', *literae humaniores* or humane letters, the study of the literature, history and ideas of the ancient world in the original Greek and Latin texts. But the word 'humanism' itself was unknown to both the ancient world and the Renaissance. It was first coined in its German form *Humanismus* as late as 1808 by a German educationalist F. J. Niethammer in a debate about the place of the classics in secondary education, and first applied to the Renaissance by George Voigt in a study published in 1859 with the title, *The Revival of Classical Antiquity or the First Century of Humanism* – the year before Burckhardt's famous *Civilisation of the Renaissance in Italy*.

If humanism is a later usage, a word that was in use by students in Italy at the end of the fifteenth century was *umanista*, humanist, a slang term to describe a teacher of the classical languages and literature, as *legista* was used to describe a teacher of law. The Renaissance term for what they taught was *studia humanitatis*, which we translate as 'the humanities', and which in the fifteenth century stood for a group of subjects, grammar, rhetoric, history, literature and moral philosophy, the study of which involved the reading of Latin texts from classical pre-Christian times, including Latin translations from the Greek and, less commonly, original Greek texts as well.

This was the New Learning, as Englishmen like Thomas More and Colet called it, the recovery or rebirth of classical antiquity with which more than anything else the Renaissance is identified and from which it takes its name. What nineteenth-century historians like Voigt and Burckhardt did was to apply the word humanism to the new attitudes and beliefs which they associated with the revival of classical learning and which they described as Renaissance humanism.

2

This is a complicated story, but one which I had to set out because it leads to the first and one of the most protracted controversies surrounding the word humanism. Few works of historiography have had a greater impact than Burckhardt's *Civilisation of the Renaissance in Italy* which established the identification of the Renaissance with humanism, a cliché endlessly repeated in every college and school text book and in every guide book – and as vigorously rejected by a majority of twentieth-century historians specializing in the period. Why?

To anyone following the controversy it has looked at times as if Burckhardt's critics would be content with nothing less than expunging both 'Renaissance' and 'humanism' from the historians' vocabulary and treating the conjunction of the two as a mythical creation comparable with the unicorn and the hippogryph. In recent years, however, historians have shown less interest in continuing to debate large generalizations about the Renaissance than in going back to the evidence and extending it by the detailed study of neglected texts, which can often produce new and surprising insights. As the controversy has died down, if only from exhaustion, a number of tentative conclusions have crystallized, two of which provide the best way into the first phase of the humanist tradition which I want to examine.

The first is that the word Renaissance has come to be used as a label for so wide and diverse an historical period, the early modern history of Europe between, say, 1350 and 1600, that it cannot be given a unified character. The old characterization of the Renaissance as the age of humanism is no longer acceptable. A great deal was happening in Europe in those 250 years which cannot possibly be described as humanism. As one set of examples, let me point to the Reformation, the Counter Reformation and the wars of religion. As another, to the medieval tradition of scholastic philosophy and the study of Aristotle which, far from being replaced by humanistic studies, not only survived but flourished in the universities and contributed not a little (some would argue, more than humanism) to the revolutionary changes in scientific thought which begin with Copernicus and Galileo.

This does not mean that the New Learning and the attempt to recover the lost world of antiquity which are the core of Renaissance humanism are unimportant. The fact that the word for that rebirth, Renaissance, has come to stand for the whole period of early modern European history supplies the best possible proof to the contrary. But if one is going to say anything about the Renaissance in its original sense as the revival of interest in the ancient world, it is necessary to specify the time and place one is referring to, and to recognize, for example, that this began in Italy a century before the rest of Europe; and that there are important differences between Italian humanism and the Christian humanism of Erasmus, characteristic of northern Europe, and between both and that of Rabelais or Montaigne in France.

The second conclusion is that there was no abrupt or easily defined break between the Middle Ages and the Renaissance. Other medieval habits of thought besides scholasticism survived into the sixteenth century in many parts of Europe, and *vice versa* there were precedents in the Middle Ages for Renaissance ways of looking at man and his world.

After all, the language of the Church and of educated people for a thousand years had been Latin, and the achievements of antiquity were far too impressive for the Middle Ages to be able to ignore them. They depended upon the ancient world for much of their knowledge, from Roman law to mathematics (Euclid) and astronomy (Ptolemy). No poets were more widely read in medieval Europe than Ovid and Vergil; and it was the latter whom Dante chose to make his guide in the first part of the *Divine Comedy*, the supreme representation of the medieval view of life. The medieval Church had to come to terms with Greek philosophy: the most famous, though by no means the last of many attempts to do so was Thomas Aquinas' *Summa*, the reconciliation of Christian teaching with Aristotle which provided the basis of scholasticism and outlasted the Renaissance. Even before Aquinas two previous classical revivals have been identified – the Carolingian of the ninth century, and the so-called proto-Renaissance of the twelfth century.

But to recognize what the art historian Erwin Panofsky[3] calls the thousand ties linking the age of the Renaissance to the Middle Ages does not mean taking continuity to mean identity. There was, to take the question I have just been discussing, a crucial difference between the way the ancient world was viewed in earlier centuries and the way it came to be viewed, first of all in Italy, in the fourteenth and fifteenth centuries. The Middle Ages had been able to appropriate what they wanted from classical antiquity precisely because they felt no sense of separateness from the ancient world. But whatever they borrowed from antiquity, whether in art, mythology, literature or philosophy, they incorporated into their own entirely different Christian system of belief and altered its original significance to fit this without any sense of anachronism. It was only with Petrarch and the Italian humanists of the fourteenth and fifteenth centuries that the world of antiquity came to be seen no longer as a storehouse to be plundered, but as a separate civilization in its own right. Instead of the sense of casual familiarity with the ancient world which the Middle Ages had felt, the Renaissance saw it for the first time in an historical perspective, as remote, unfamiliar and fascinating. Their efforts were devoted not to incorporating particular features of it but trying to penetrate it as a coherent and very different world which they admired as immeasurably superior to their own.

It was the Italian humanists of the fourteenth and fifteenth centuries who developed the idea of a 'renaissance' of antiquity and invented the term 'the middle age' to describe the gulf which separated them from the ancient world they claimed to be restoring. Making his first visit to Rome in 1337, and moved 'beyond words' by the impression of its ruins, Petrarch reversed the accepted concept of history, replacing the

Cyzici ante templi frontispicium hinc inde pro por
ttonibus et eximia arte pampinere utribus & uitis

ttcum uel pronaon habentes quinas hinc inde parietibus
ornatissimae columnas.

traditional contrast between heathen darkness and the Christian age inaugurated by the incarnation of Christ, with one between an age of glory identified with the Roman Republic and Empire and the dark ages of Christian Rome, a darkness now to be dispelled by the revival of the lost arts of the past, a programme taken up with enthusiasm by his successors.

There is no doubt that they believed this, and if they exaggerated (as they certainly did), their sense of a new departure remains as an historical fact even when the degree of continuity with the Middle Ages has been restored by subsequent research. And not for the last time, as we shall see when we come to talk of the later classical revival of the time of Winckelmann and Goethe, the rediscovery of the world of antiquity released new energies and stimulated the imagination to the discovery of

11 Temple of Cyzicus, from the sketchbooks of Cyriac of Ancona, copied *c.* 1475 by Bartolommeo Fonzio

new truths and the invention of new forms besides recovering much of value from the past that had been lost or distorted.

3

As a rough generalization, Western thought has treated man and the cosmos in three distinct modes. The first, the supernatural or the transcendental, has focused on God, treating man as a part of the Divine Creation. A second, the natural or the scientific, has focused on Nature and treats man as part of the natural order like other organisms. The third, the humanistic, has focused on Man, and on human experience as the starting point for man's knowledge of himself, of God and of Nature.

The first of these modes was dominant in the Middle Ages, when Western thought had a special relationship with theology. Although the humanistic, which has a similar close relationship with literature and the arts, history and social thought, could draw upon the philosophical traditions of the ancient world, its modern version only took shape during the Renaissance period; and the scientific later still, in the seventeenth century. This is an outrageous simplification but a useful one, subject to two provisions. The first is that the distinction is to be taken as one between three tendencies which can be combined in a variety of ways, not as hard and fast lines of demarcation. The second is that it is not to be taken as another version of Comte's law of three stages, with the humanistic superseding the theological and then in turn being superseded by the scientific. Since the seventeenth century all three have

12 Library designed by Michelozzo, Florence

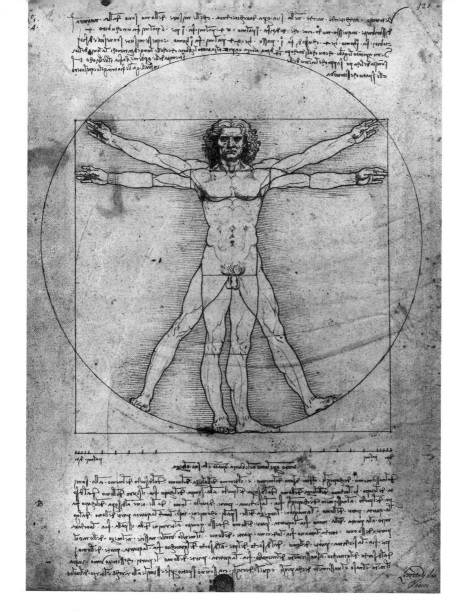

continued to be represented and to attract adherents, their relations
fluctuating between competitive claims to a monopoly of truth and
different forms of coexistence.

An individualistic variety of views was characteristic of humanism
from the beginning of the Renaissance, as it had been of the ancient
world. Human experience does not lend itself to the authoritative claims
of either religion or science. But if no two humanists were likely to agree
in their view of a question, what is distinctive is the range of topics which
they thought it important to discuss and the style in which they debated
them, frequently in dialogue form. 'There are fools', Petrarch wrote in
the middle of the fourteenth century, 'who seek to understand the secrets

17

of nature and the far more difficult secrets of God, with supercilious pride, instead of accepting them in humble faith. They cannot approach them, let alone reach them.'[4] What man could do – and Montaigne was to echo Petrarch two hundred years later at the end of the Renaissance – was to turn to the exploration of himself and the riches of human experience.

One of the great attractions of classical Greek thought was that it was man- rather than God-centred. Socrates was particularly revered because, as Cicero said, he brought philosophy down from heaven to earth. The constant demand of the humanists was for philosophy to become a school of human life, addressing itself to the common problems of humanity.

This accounts for the sharpness with which they attacked the scholastic philosophy for its preoccupation with logical categories and metaphysical questions, its abstract reasoning remote from ordinary human life. The scholastics, Petrarch complained, were always prepared to tell us things which 'even if they were true, would not contribute anything whatsoever' to enrich our lives – while remaining indifferent to such vital questions as 'man's nature, the purposes for which we are born and whereunto we travel'. In place of scholastic abstractions men should turn their minds to the moral, psychological and social questions which had always been at the heart of the rhetorical as opposed to the philosophical tradition. In his *De remediis* Petrarch himself dealt with more than 250 commonplace situations in which human beings might be tempted either to despair or elation, offering advice on how best to cope with the emotional crises of life. The last thing the Renaissance humanists wanted to do was to replace the scholastic with another system of philosophical thought. Instead they aimed at reviving a role which scholastic (but not classical) philosophy had neglected.

4

There is no simple explanation of why the Renaissance, in the sense of a rekindling of interest in the ancient world, should have begun in Italy a century before it spread to the rest of Europe. But two obvious factors stand out. One is that much of the history of antiquity had been played out on Italian soil, in Rome where the ruins of the Forum, the Colosseum and the Baths still bore silent witness to its power; in the Greek-speaking cities of the south like Syracuse; in the countryside of central and northern Italy where antique statues, coins and inscriptions were constantly turned up by the ploughman.

The other was the exceptional development of the Italian cities as a result of commercial expansion. Florence, Genoa, and Venice had become the economic leaders of Europe, and by the year 1300 there were twenty-three cities in north and central Italy with a population of

28,000 or more, the majority of them city-republics in a feudal world of peasants and monarchies. This relatively high proportion of the population living in towns, with an unusual degree of autonomy and a corresponding involvement in trade, industry and politics – even when it expressed itself in factions and feuds – acted as a forcing house for urban culture and produced a class of educated laymen with a self-confidence hardly known elsewhere in Europe,[5] except in Flanders where similar conditions prevailed. It is true that in the late thirteenth and early fourteenth centuries most of the city-states (though not Florence or Venice) came under the rule of single families and that in the mid-fourteenth century (like the rest of Europe) they suffered economic decline and the loss of a third of their population from the Black Death – so that in 1400 the Italian population was well below that of 1300. But the tradition of an educated laity and the vitality of urban life survived and were essential conditions for the spread of humanism. As Peter Burke puts it: 'No cities, no Renaissance.'[6]

. Of course we are talking about a handful of people in what today we should regard as a small town. The population of Venice, Milan and Naples in the fifteenth century hardly exceeded 100,000, Florence and Bologna no more than 50–60,000. Rome, with a population of around 25,000, was a local market-town in 1400 and was only turned into the capital of the Renaissance by the Popes in the latter part of the fifteenth

14 Prospect of Florence

century. Other centres of Renaissance humanism and art – Urbino, Ferrara and Mantua – never had more than 20–30,000 inhabitants. But size – as the other contemporary example of the Low Countries or that of fifth-century Athens shows – is no index of achievement. Peter Burke, making a rough count of the creative élite of Italy between 1420 and 1540 – humanists, writers, artists, architects, musicians and scientists – gives a figure of 600.[7] Enlarge that figure to take account of an earlier generation and it would still be well short of a thousand. Add those who cannot be identified, and then those to whom their writing and art appealed – the all-important patrons and clients, the Medici, the Este family of Ferrara, the Venetian patricians, above all the Popes; the amateurs, the dilettanti and hangers-on – and it is still a group of a few thousand, spread over a couple of centuries. Yet their achievements and impact on posterity have few equals, the solid basis of that myth of the Renaissance which sceptically-minded historians have chipped at but failed to demolish.

Among Burke's 600, the humanists number no more than a hundred, and this conforms to the modern usage of the term by historians of the Renaissance, confining it to men versed in the knowledge of Latin, less commonly of Greek as well, who used their skill to make a living as lecturers, teachers, tutors in noble or wealthy families, secretaries responsible for official correspondence and speeches in the Papal curia and other courts and chancelleries. Through them and their writings there spread amongst the educated classes of the Italian cities an enthusiasm and taste for the ancient Mediterranean world of which they felt themselves the heirs. Out of this in turn developed a new mixture of culture, not an imitation but a new style of thought and feeling, not least

15 The ducal palace of Urbino built by Federigo II of Montelfeltro (1422–82), who successfully combined the roles of condottiere, ruler and humanist

of looking, which later came to be seen as distinctive and to which the nineteenth century gave the name humanism.

The ability to write a purer and more elegant form of Latin, modelled on authors like Cicero, to which the humanists themselves attached so much importance, has left behind a great quantity of unoriginal and unreadable prize compositions. But to lay the foundations of humanistic scholarship was a lasting achievement. From amateurish beginnings in the thirteenth century, gradually building up a large fund of knowledge, the humanists recovered lost texts from monastic libraries; developed the techniques of textual criticism to emend corrupt editions and created classical archaeology with the systematic study of Roman remains. They greatly improved Western knowledge not only of Greek as a language, but, through the translation of Greek texts, of Greek thought and literature for those who knew only Latin, producing a complete translation of Plato's works for the first time and even in the case of Aristotle more accurate versions than the Middle Ages had possessed.

When one reflects on how much in civilization depends on the ability to determine whether documentary records, the statements or claims

16 John Argyropoulos (1415–87), Byzantine scholar who taught Greek and Greek philosophy at the University of Florence

they make, are genuine or false – to distinguish the authentic from forgeries – it is possible to recognize how great a contribution was made by those who first created the tradition and established the standards of philological scholarship.

But the *studia humanitatis* (the study of the humanities), like the equally misleading word rhetoric which formed a part of them, was not concerned only with the linguistic and textual techniques of studying Latin and Greek texts. It was concerned with their subject matter as well – with the poetry of Vergil (and later of Homer); with the histories of Livy and Tacitus (later of Thucydides); with the discussion of Stoicism and moral philosophy in Cicero (later with Plato's dialogues). From the humanists' letters it is still possible to recapture the excitement of exploring a new continent, building up piece by piece the image of a very different civilization from their own, seen as a coherent and completed cycle passing from obscurity through empire – first Greek, then Roman – to decline and breakdown.

As the ancient world gradually took shape out of their studies, it came to be recognized as an alternative source of models not only for rhetoric and literature, the arts of painting, sculpture and architecture, but for the most important art of all, that of living, both private (the art of bearing up under adversity) and public (the art of statecraft).

5

Of course there were pedants among the humanists as well as time-servers who used their talents to flatter the powerful. They were as quarrelsome, touchy and jealous a community as any academic or literary group of today in New York, London or Paris, forever taking offence and writing letters full of complaints and criticisms of each other. Let me briefly introduce you to three or four of the outstanding figures among the earlier generation.

Petrarch (1304–74), born in exile and seventeen years old when Dante died, stands in a unique position. If he was not the first to show an interest in humanistic studies, he brought humanism to life with all the flair of a great innovator. He knew more about the Latin classics than any medieval man before him; he discovered in Verona the lost text of Cicero's letters, produced an emended text of Livy and restored Latin to the status of a living language by writing a whole series of original works. Among them are biographies modelled on Plutarch and collections of letters, which provide a fascinating and complex self-portrait of a man who has been called the first intellectual. Other studies were devoted to trying to reconcile humanistic studies with Christianity, to attacking the dominant scholastic philosophy and to invectives against his critics – all in Latin. He also wrote poems in the vernacular which remain among the finest in Italian literature.

Salutati, my second figure, had none of the genius of Petrarch. His own Latin writings are pedestrian. But Petrarch, while he enjoyed an eminence which brought him the friendship of popes and kings, was a solitary, rootless man who left no school behind him. Salutati, born in 1330, had other gifts. He combined a passion for the classics with the Stoic belief that this should find expression in the active life of public affairs. From 1375 until his death in 1406 he was Chancellor of Florence in turbulent years, beginning with the revolt of the *Ciompi* (the wool-workers) and overshadowed by a series of wars with Milan in which only the death of Giangaleazzo Visconti in 1402 saved the republic from disaster. The heart and soul of Florentine resistance and the man responsible for using his skill as a Latinist to conduct the city's diplomatic correspondence, on which so much depended, he turned the Chancellorship into a position of real power. The greatest enemy of Florence, Giangaleazzo, is reported to have said that Salutati's letters were worth a thousand horsemen.

No less important, Salutati made Florence the focus of Italian humanism in the first half of the fifteenth century, collecting and inspiring a circle of younger men to continue the tradition Petrarch had begun. His appointment in 1397 of the Byzantine scholar Manuel Chrysoloras to teach Greek at the expense of the Commune was a turning point in Greek studies. A great teacher, in three years Chrysoloras gave to a generation of students not only a grounding in Greek but a lifelong enthusiasm for the study of the classics.

Among those Chrysoloras influenced was Leonardo Bruni. Bruni (1369–1444) was a poor student who established himself by his mastery of Latin as a secretary in the Papal curia. He returned to Florence in 1415 and never left it until his death, becoming Salutati's successor as the focus of the city's political and literary life and, eventually, as Chancellor. He wrote a history of the Florentine people, from Roman to contemporary times, which is a landmark in Renaissance historiography, and in spite of his part in public affairs, he found the time to turn out a whole series of translations from Greek into Latin of Xenophon, Plato, Plutarch, Demosthenes and Aristotle.

My last figure comes closer, perhaps, than any other fifteenth-century figure to the Renaissance ideal of *l'uomo universale*. Leon Battista Alberti (1404–72) was born in exile, the bastard son of one of the wealthiest Florentine families which had lost out in the city's perennial faction fights. Athlete, humanist scholar, scientist, mathematician, musician, architect, cryptographer, a master equally of Latin and Italian, by his writings on painting and architecture he transformed the practice of the visual arts and founded art theory.

As Salutati and Bruni are the representatives of what has been called civic humanism, Alberti's career illustrates the fusion between humanism and the arts. The pioneer in moving towards a more realistic

style of painting was Giotto; but when he died in 1337 he left no
successors. It was not until a century later, in the 1430s when Alberti
spent much time in Florence, that Masaccio (1401–c.1428), Donatello
(1386–1466) and Brunelleschi (1377–1446) picked up where Giotto had
left off and carried further the revolution in representation which he had
begun. It was Alberti who systematized the theory of perspective which
Brunelleschi had invented, and produced in *Della Pittura* (1436) a work
which was to have an enormous influence on patrons and painters. His
dialogues *Della famiglia* and *Della tranquillità dell'animo*, which deal with
moral questions, were followed by a preoccupation with the physical
remains of antiquity and the study of Vitruvius, leading to his own
architectural treatise, *De re aedificatoria* (completed 1452, published
1485), which became essential reading for architects well into the
eighteenth century. Packed with technical guidance, it laid stress both on
the social function of architecture (a first essay in town planning) and on
a theory of proportions derived from the natural principles of harmony
which applied throughout the universe. As proof that his theories could
be translated into practice he designed and built some of the most
striking examples of Renaissance architecture, in Rimini, Mantua and
Florence.

   The Florentine humanism of which Alberti and Bruni had been a part
in the 1430s changed out of recognition in the second half of the fifteenth
century. Under the patronage of Cosimo (1389–1464) and Lorenzo de
Medici (1449–92) the city became a centre for very different forms of
philosophy and art dominated by Platonist and Neoplatonist ideas. Its
central figure was Marsilio Ficino (1433–99), the leading spirit of the
Platonic Academy founded by the Medici, the translator of Plato's
dialogues into Latin and the author of the influential *Platonic theology
concerning the immortality of the soul* (1469–74). The artistic equivalents of

this Neoplatonist synthesis of Christianity and humanism are Botticelli's two famous pictures, the *Primavera* and the *Birth of Venus*. Then, with the death of Lorenzo in 1492, the episode of Savonarola, the invasion of Italy by the French and the beginning of the Italian wars in 1494, Florence entered upon a troubled period in which she could still produce a Machiavelli, a Guicciardini and a Vasari, but saw her place as the capital of the Italian Renaissance taken by a rebuilt Rome and a Papacy restored by a succession of humanist popes, of whom Pius II (Aeneas Sylvius Piccolomini, 1458–64) and Julius II (1503–13) are the best known.

In the meantime, printing had opened a wholly new prospect for the humanists and Italy (where the first printed books date from the 1460s) rapidly became the most important publishing country in Europe, with Venice pre-eminent. Venice was the last of the Italian republics to preserve its independence; and with the most famous Italian university, Padua, in its territory, with such a publisher as Aldus Manutius (?1450–1515), famous for his printing of Greek texts, and such artists as the Bellinis, Titian, Giorgione, Tintoretto and Veronese, it produced yet another and final version of Italian humanism. It was to Venice that Erasmus came in 1506 to work at the Aldine Press with Aldus Manutius, and in Venice that Albrecht Dürer, who opened northern eyes to the classical world recovered by Italian artists and Italian humanists, first had his own eyes opened.

The northern Renaissance overlaps with the later phase of the Italian. The first generation of northerners to study in Italy had travelled there in the 1480s and 1490s,[8] and northern humanism came to fruition in the

18 The church of San Sebastiano at Mantua, by Alberti

early sixteenth century. 1508 was the year in which Greek was first regularly taught in the University of Paris. 1516 was the year which saw the publication of Thomas More's *Utopia* and Erasmus' Greek New Testament; the three humanist colleges of Corpus Christi, Oxford, Christ's College and St John's at Cambridge were created at the same time. In the 1520s Budé, the greatest Greek scholar of his day in France, persuaded Francis I, the humanist monarch in whose service Leonardo da Vinci died at Amboise, to found the Bibliothèque Royale, followed by the Collège de France in 1530, two institutions which have remained among the intellectual glories of France for four centuries.

Christian humanism was to be found not only in the Low Countries and France (the circle round Lefebvre d'Etaples in Paris); but in Germany, where it inspired Luther's chief lieutenant, Philipp Melanchthon, and Johann Reuchlin, the pioneer of Hebrew studies. In Spain the Primate, Cardinal Ximenes, founder of the humanist university of Alcalá, provided the funds for a six-volume edition of the Bible printed in the original languages of Hebrew and Greek, with the Latin translation of the Vulgate alongside. But northern humanism was not confined to the Christian version characteristic of the early decades of the sixteenth century. The 1530s, for example, saw the publication of Rabelais' *Pantagruel* and his *Gargantua*, striking an entirely new note in the gamut of humanism, while fifty years later Montaigne provided in his *Essais* an equally original reflective postscript to a movement that had been beaten down by the violence and intolerance of the religious quarrels.

19 A Greek grammar with Latin translation edited by Constantine Lascaris and printed by Erasmus's friend Aldus Manutius in Venice 'on the last day of February 1494'

20 Guillaume Budé, the leading French humanist (about 1520)

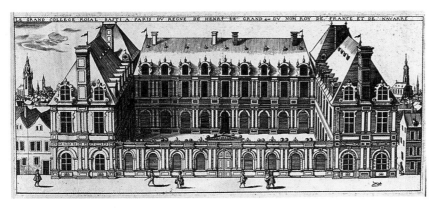

6

One of the favourite topics of humanist discussion was the relative merits of the active and the contemplative life. If answers differed widely, the fact that the superiority of the contemplative life could be openly questioned is striking. The contrast which Bruni drew between the 'life of business' (*vita negotiosa*) and the 'life of idleness' (*vita otiosa*) associated with monasticism – a contrast natural to an urban patriciate like that of Florence or Venice, active in trade, finance and politics – was sharpened by the life and death struggle in the early decades of the fifteenth century to defend the Florentine republic against the Milanese despotism of the Visconti. From that struggle sprang civic humanism, the combination of city-state politics and classical history which saw the citizen's service to the city-state as the highest good and led Bruni to compare Florence with Republican Rome and Periclean Athens. 'I am persuaded', Alberti wrote, 'that man was not born to pine away in indolence but to become active in magnificent and large affairs.'

A second theme, again reviving classical concepts condemned by St Augustine, was the clash between the caprice of Fortune (no longer seen in terms of Christian Providence) and the *Virtù* of the man who refused to yield to it (no longer seen in terms of Christian virtue). Humanists like Alberti insisted that men, if they were bold enough, could subdue Fortune. This emphasis on man's creative powers, his freedom to fashion his own life, produced that interest in the individual personality and the heightened awareness of the self which Burckhardt saw as the distinctive mark of the Italian Renaissance, reflected in the growing number of portraits, self-portraits, biographies and autobiographies, executed for the first time in a realistic, no longer in a symbolical or allegorical, style.

Burckhardt in *The Civilisation of the Renaissance in Italy* (1860) drew a picture of that society as self-assertive, competitive, bent upon achievement and avid for glory and immortality. This is another familiar theme of humanist discourse. In answer to the combined condemnation of the pursuit of worldly honour and glory by St

Augustine, Thomas Aquinas and Pope Innocent III, Alberti wrote (echoing Petrarch), 'Nature has instilled a great desire for praise and glory in everyone who is not completely listless and dull of mind.'

This development of an independent secular scale of values derived from the rediscovery of the ancient pre-Christian past found expression in a more acute sense of history, no longer seen as the working out of a providential plan but as the product of human efforts and failures. The first attempts to give expression to this by writers like Bruni and Poggio – both fifteenth-century chancellors of Florence – broke with the episodic form of the chroniclers and made the crucial step to explaining the flow of events as a continual process. They were still hobbled, however, by the desire to assimilate their narratives to classical models and to defend republicanism against monarchy. It was only in the final phase of the Italian Renaissance, in the sixteenth century, that Guicciardini and Machiavelli showed what humanist historical and political writing could achieve at its best. Both remained republicans in the Florentine tradition of civic humanism, committed to the supreme value of liberty but without illusions about the character of the times in which they lived. Guicciardini's *History of Italy* was ranked by Gibbon with Thucydides; Machiavelli, who wrote in the preface of his Discourses on Livy that he was opening 'a road as yet untrodden by man', displayed a boldness in the analysis of power which has never been surpassed.

Machiavelli (1469–1527) is a figure whom it is impossible to leave out of the humanist tradition and equally impossible to fit in. He remains as original and troubling as he appeared to his contemporaries, but rooted in a humanism of which he was the sharpest critic. Like Guicciardini (1483–1540), he needed no convincing of the value of liberty and self-government, was an enemy of oppression and corruption, and passionately devoted to the Florence which he served as diplomat and soldier. But his observation of men's behaviour and his reading of history convinced him that if a kingdom or republic was to avoid disaster its rulers must be prepared to go to any lengths in dissimulation, deceit and force – employing, in his famous metaphor, 'the ferocity of the lion and the cunning of the fox' – when the safety and freedom of their native country were at stake.

Machiavelli's originality lies in combining loftiness of aim with an unhesitating insistence that this not only justifies but demands readiness to use the most reprehensible means to achieve it. This originality was enhanced by the clear and vivid style in which he wrote. He had a gift for paradox and an inner compulsion to push his observations and thoughts to a logical conclusion, producing dazzling generalizations, often on too narrow a base of evidence. But far from being a cold and cynical opportunist who made evil his good, he was an ardent, generous man who was moved – as his biographer Roberto Ridolfi puts it – 'by his anguished despair of ever seeing virtue triumphant and his tragic sense of evil'.⁹

7

What still gives Machiavelli's writing its power is its focussing on the problem that lies at the heart of all political action: the relation between power and conscience, *virtù* and virtue, ends and means; his refusal to accept the conventional answers and his insistence, nonetheless, that an answer has to be found. Characteristically, he maintained that Christianity had elevated the wrong values since it had 'assigned as man's highest good humility, abnegation and contempt for mundane things', the effect of which had been to hand the world over 'as a prey to the wicked'. The old religion of Republican Rome had glorified the civic virtues and so helped to sustain political freedom; the Christian religion 'has glorified humble and contemplative men' and thus helped to bring about the corruption of the Commonwealth.¹⁰

Going beyond the political context in which Machiavelli discusses it, this raises the question of the compatibility of the Christian religion, not just with Machiavelli's highly individual version (which most humanists repudiated), but with the much wider and varied spectrum of humanist views to be found in the Renaissance period in Italy and later in other parts of Europe as well.

The answer appears to be that before the middle years of the sixteenth century, when the earlier confidence of the humanists was turning to disillusionment, few would have gone as far as Machiavelli – or felt any need to. From the beginning, the direction of their thought had been towards a more secular view of human life focused on 'this' rather than 'the other' world of the medieval imagination, an historical in place of a metaphysical view. This was reinforced by the rediscovery of the philosophical ideas of antiquity – for example, those of the Stoics or the cult of the goddess Fortuna.

As early as 1337 when Petrarch wrote the first draft of his treatise *On Famous Men*, he ignored completely the medieval pantheon of saints and martyrs and took his examples from the pagan heroes of antiquity. A hundred years later (in 1452) Giannozzo Manetti (1396–1459) produced another treatise, *On The Dignity and Excellence of Man*, which was a point-by-point rebuttal of Innocent III's famous *Misery of Man*, and in which Manetti expressed his belief in man's 'unmeasurable dignity and excellence' and in 'the extraordinary endowments and rare privileges' of his nature.

To us there is no getting away from the conflict between the Augustinian picture of the sinful condition of human existence and the impossibility of man, a fallen creature, being able to achieve anything without God's aid, and the Renaissance view of man able by his own

powers to aspire to the highest excellence, shape his own life and win fame by his achievements. But for the humanists themselves this rarely posed a problem; the majority continued to take their Christian faith for granted and to feel no need to accommodate their classical enthusiasm to it.

For the few who were troubled, there were two ways open to them, Neoplatonism and Biblical humanism, which in different ways represent the religious element in Renaissance humanism.

It can hardly be an accident that Neoplatonism began to flourish in Florence in the second half of the fifteenth century, after the rise of the Medici to power had undermined the city's liberties. The ideal of the active life vigorously preached by the civic humanists of the first half of the century was now replaced by the contemplative and mystical ideals of Marsilio Ficino and the Platonic Academy which enjoyed the patronage of the Medici. Cosimo de' Medici commissioned Ficino to produce for the first time a complete translation into Latin of Plato's works (completed in 1484) and Lorenzo encouraged him to produce his own philosophical work, *The Platonic theology concerning the immortality of the soul*. Ficino emphasized the close kinship between the Platonic philosophy and the Christian religion, reinforcing this by drawing upon the Neoplatonic tradition of Proclus and Plotinus and the Hermetic Writings (the *Corpus Hermeticum*), a system of mystical and gnostic ideas attributed (falsely) to the mythical Greek god Hermes Trismegistus, who in turn was identified with the Egyptian God Thoth. Ficino's aim was to bring out the essential unity of all these different religious traditions, seeing them as parallel paths to a truth connected at source in the ancient world. With this faith in the unity of religious belief was linked (for example in the writings of the much admired Cardinal Nicholas of Cusa) that belief in harmony and proportion as the underlying principles of the universe which made so strong an appeal to Renaissance minds, and with both of which man could identify himself through the supreme human activity of contemplation.

There is no doubt about the irreconcilability of the Neoplatonist emphasis on the contemplative life and the civic humanists' on the active; but there is equally no doubt about the claim both could make to be considered humanists. Ficino drew his inspiration from antiquity as much as Salutati and Bruni did, albeit from the Hellenistic age rather than Republican Rome; and in the hierarchy of the universe he placed man at the centre of creation, the link between all that had been created, belonging to the lower order of matter but capable of rising higher still to unity with God himself. It was this capacity of union with the divine that Ficino's pupil, the young Pico, lord of Mirandola (1463–1494), celebrated in his famous oration *On the Dignity of Man* (1486).

This complex of humanistic ideas, ramifying from Neoplatonism through mysticism and the Renaissance fascination with magic, astrology and the figure of the Magus (which Frances Yates[11] has explored) to Pythagorean number symbolism, mythology and allegory, had a profound impact on European art and literature – not least Elizabethan literature – which lasted well into the seventeenth century.

A quite different way of approaching religious truth was offered by Biblical humanism. It was the possibility of applying the methods of humanistic scholarship to the text of the Bible and the patristic writings of the Church Fathers which first attracted the northern humanists to learn from the Italians. Indeed, it was an Italian, Lorenzo Valla (1407–57), who in his efforts to reconcile Christian and humanist studies opened the way for Erasmus. Erasmus himself (c.1466–1536) had been brought up by the Brethren of the Common Life, an order of devout laymen in the Low Countries who turned away from both theology and mysticism to devote themselves to following the example of Christ's life in the world. It was this simple, undogmatic and ethical view of Christianity, set out in Thomas à Kempis' *Imitation of Christ*, which Erasmus absorbed and retained for the rest of his life. He found no difficulty in combining this religious faith with a mastery of classical literature, both Latin and Greek, which made him the most famous humanist scholar of his time. He turned his scholarship to producing a critical edition of the Greek New Testament and a new translation into Latin, both of which, thanks to the printing press, were widely circulated throughout Europe, called the authority of the Vulgate into question, and provided a major weapon for the Protestant reformers. Erasmus believed that the surest way to recapture the pure and uncorrupted spirit of Christ's original teaching was through the scholarly editing of the documents of the Early Church and the translation of the Bible into English, French and German.

Biblical humanism, which attracted some of the finest and most devout minds in France, Germany, England and the Low Countries, provides impressive evidence that such men felt no barrier between an undogmatic, devotional form of Christianity and the humanist

24–5 Cranach's portraits of Luther (1525) and Philipp Melanchthon

enthusiasm for the New Learning. As Professor Kristeller puts it, while Renaissance thought was more man-centred and more secular than medieval thought, it was not necessarily less religious.[12]

The tragedy was that this movement was overtaken and swamped by the quarrel between the more militant Reformers and the Papacy which widened the differences to the point where everyone was forced into one camp or the other. A middle position became untenable, and arguments over beliefs were hopelessly entangled with struggles for power, political ambitions, social tensions and emergent national feelings.

It was argued at the time, and has been ever since, that it needed the uncompromising stand taken by Luther to make any impression on a corrupt Church and force the issue of reform to a conclusion which produced not only the separate and reformed Protestant Churches, but the reforms of the Counter Reformation within the Church itself. This may well be so, but the question whether there was an alternative version of European history is a Serbonian bog in which it would be as unwise as it is unnecessary for us to enter. The only point I wish to establish in the context of these lectures is the effect of the quarrel on the humanist tradition in northern Europe. For this was one of the most important sources of the Reform movement and many Christian humanists initially shared the aim of reforming the Church. Both Luther himself (1483–1546) and Philipp Melanchthon (1497–1560), the outstanding humanist scholar who became his chief lieutenant, never abandoned their view that the mastery of classical studies and their application to the Bible, in which Erasmus had been a pioneer, were the key to a recovery of the original uncorrupted teaching of Christ. Moreover, Luther's rejection of the mediatory role of the priesthood and his insistence on the direct relationship between the individual human being and God could well be seen as a natural development of humanism, as could his insistence on the translation of the Bible into the vernacular.

There were, however, two stumbling blocks, one or other of which, in some cases both, held back the majority of Christian humanists from following Luther, at least outside Germany where his strong appeal to nascent German national feeling had no comparable effect. One was the increasing lengths to which Luther was prepared to go in abandoning the traditional practices as well as beliefs of the Church, finally in outright separation from it. The other was the revival by Luther, and even more vehemently by Calvin (1509–64), of an uncompromising insistence on man's corrupt and sinful nature, capable of being redeemed only by the intervention of divine grace – a view as incompatible, in Erasmus' view, with the spirit of Christ's teaching as it was with humanism. The bitter divisions which resulted put an end to the earlier promise of Christian humanism, and cost Erasmus his influence and Thomas More his life.

8

Whatever else humanists might disagree about, all, including Luther and Melanchthon as well as Erasmus, agreed on the importance of education. A knowledge of Latin and Greek was the key necessary to provide access to the experience and thought of the ancient world.

Old Italian town schools were revived, and enlightened princes established others, at which their own as well as the children of leading court and burgher families were taught by humanists, the best of whom were eagerly sought after. The two most famous of these schools, which were copied in other countries, were the one known as *La Giocosa*, which Vittorino da Feltre established for the Gonzaga family, lords of Mantua, and where he taught from 1423 to 1446; and that which Guarino da Verona (who had studied Greek under Chrysolaras in Florence and later followed him to Byzantium) created for Niccolò d'Este, the lord of Ferrara, in 1429.

If man lived in society, especially in societies as small and intense as those of Italian cities, then his education had to develop his social as well as his mental qualities. In an age of violence he had to learn to control his passions; in an age when power was exercised brutally, to learn the art of courtesy; in a competitive age, to prefer the gamesmanship of the amateur to that of the professional. In an age which exalted excellence and was not tolerant of mediocrity, the aim was the general education of an élite rather than the production of specialists, the ideal *'uomo universale'*, a Leonardo, an Alberti, a Michelangelo.

The total number of these schools was of course small in relation to the total population, but the humanists' concentration on the education of a governing class, whether princely or republican, bore fruit in the formative effect it had on their pupils' subsequent attitudes. In the fifteenth century it ceased to be sufficient for young men of ruling families to be trained solely in chivalry and the arts of war: the Renaissance ideal required them to be proficient in the Arts (music, for example) and Letters as well as Arms. A string of manuals on the education of princes show how seriously this was taken – and with good reason in an age when monarchs could make or mar the happiness of their peoples, including changing their religion, as Henry VIII did.[13]

The greatest of English monarchs, Queen Elizabeth I, was a paragon of humanist education; her tutor Roger Ascham went on to write the best known educational treatise, *The Schoolmaster*, in a country where the establishment of grammar schools ensured the continuation of the humanist tradition down to the mid-twentieth century. The most famous of these was St Paul's School in London, founded in 1512 by More's and Erasmus' friend John Colet for teaching 'children of all nacions and countries indifferently to the noumber of cliij' [153]. Twenty-five years later, Johannes Sturm started another variant of the humanist tradition in education when he gave the Greek name *gymnasium* to the Latin grammar school he opened in Strassburg and directed for more than forty years. Ironically, the one thing Luther and Ignatius Loyola, the founder of the Jesuits, had in common they both took from the humanists and left as a legacy to their own followers: their belief in the importance of schooling and their insistence on the value of a classical education.

The universities were a different story. Except where there were new foundations (see p. 26 above), they remained strongholds of scholastic theology and Aristotelianism, and of the traditional study of law and medicine, often influenced by but resistant to the New Learning. Humanism was essentially a lay movement independent of both the Church and the universities. It found more characteristic expression in informal groups, such as that which surrounded Thomas More in England, or Queen Marguerite of Navarre (1492–1549) in France, and which frequently went by the name of academies in Italy. Other groups were formed in the London Inns of Court or held together by that remarkable network of correspondence of which Erasmus' letters are but one example. To this one should add the revolutionary effect of the invention of printing, of which Erasmus was one of the first to take advantage. The texts of a great range of classical authors, Greek as well as Latin, for the first time became easily available throughout Europe. This

provided as never before the framework of an invisible college of humanist scholarship.

The central theme of humanism was the potentialities of man, his creative powers. But these powers, including the power to mould himself, were latent; they had to be awoken, brought out, educed, and the means to that end was education. The humanists saw education as the process by which man was lifted out of his natural condition to discover his *humanitas*. In the Renaissance *studia humanitatis*, grammar and rhetoric introduced the student not only to classical scholarship and the ability to write and speak effectively, but to literature, history and moral philosophy – not just the forms but the contents of the classical works they studied. It was from Homer and Thucydides, from Vergil and Cicero, that they learned the meaning of *humanitas*.

I have already spoken of the importance the humanists attached to the study of history. They laid equal stress on the study of language. Lorenzo Valla, for example, saw in the history of words a means of retracing the development of an institution and a concept – in law, for example – or of a custom and a way of life. Language was what distinguished man from all the animals, the means of social and human communication which enabled him to develop the art of living together with others.

No ambition was dearer to the early humanists than to restore Latin to the purity of classical usage. But Petrarch, who had first conceived this

26 Woodcut by Dürer designed as a printer's device for Josse Bade (Jodocus Badius Ascensianus). Bade, one of the first scholar-printers to settle in Paris, had learned the art of printing in Italy as well as Greek, which he taught at Lyons for ten years. His classical texts rivalled those of Aldus Manutius' press in Venice

27 Holbein's drawing of John Colet, English humanist and founder of St Paul's School

ambition, wrote some of his finest poems in the Tuscan vernacular, and the question of Latin versus the vernacular remained a permanent topic of dispute out of which, by the sixteenth century, the Italian language had emerged, purified in the process. It was in Italian that Machiavelli and his sixteenth-century contemporaries wrote and the same development took place in France, England and Spain. In all these countries the revival of the classics led to the flowering of the vernacular languages and was followed by a Golden Age of literature – Rabelais, Montaigne, Shakespeare, Milton, Cervantes and Camoens – permanently enriched by the recovery of the classical world but no longer dependent on Latin for its transmission.

9

Most people find it easier to identify humanism with Renaissance art than with Renaissance thought or literature – not surprisingly. But once again it is necessary to be clear what we are talking about, for there is a great deal of art of the Renaissance period, some of it of the highest quality, which has little or no connection with the humanist tradition. The most interesting case is that of the Netherlands under the rule of the Burgundian court, where in the fifteenth century Jan van Eyck, one of the greatest painters who ever lived, Hugo van der Goes, the Master of Flémalle and Rogier van der Weyden evolved a new style remarkable for its naturalism, especially in the representation of landscape, and for such innovations as painting in oil.

But while the Netherlands painters, in particular van Eyck, looked back to their own Romanesque traditions of the early Middle Ages, they did not take the further step which the Italians took (for example, Brunelleschi) when they went back beyond the Romanesque to the original Roman sources. It is this association with the revival of antiquity that justifies the use of the term 'humanist' to describe the innovatory art of the Renaissance in Italy. The revival of a feeling for classical proportions and movement in the north had to wait for Dürer a century later.

The innovators in Italy were an architect, Brunelleschi, a painter, Masaccio, and a sculptor, Donatello. There were abundant remains in Italy of classical architecture and sculpture, even a few surviving wall-paintings and mosaics – and it was through these that classical forms and classical motifs entered Italian painting. The artists' pursuit of what has been called the 'absent model' of antique art, however, never fell into the trap of mere imitation which deprived so much humanist writing in Latin of life. Far from being stifled by anxiety about authenticity, their imaginations were stimulated and released. André Chastel described Renaissance art, in its relations with the antique, as 'a gigantic enterprise of cultural pseudo-morphosis . . . In its efforts to rediscover antiquity it

28 Brunelleschi's sacristy in San Lorenzo, Florence, with two figures in bas-relief by Donatello

29 Italian money changers and bankers

30 Architectural perspective view of an ideal city (15th-century Italy)

created something quite different.' That this was already recognized at the time is shown by the letter Raphael (1483–1520) wrote to Pope Leo X in 1519: 'Rather may Your Holiness, always keeping alive the imitation of the antique, equal it and surpass it, as you in fact do with great buildings.'[14]

It was no accident that this development started in fifteenth-century Florence, where the Florentines' pride in their city was an essential part of civic humanism and led to a remarkable communal effort to embellish it in which Brunelleschi, Donatello and Masaccio were all employed. The early humanists' ideal city was given visible form in Florence, and Alberti was there to systematize for generations to come the new practice of the arts of painting, sculpture and architecture in his Treatises. Most striking of these new ways was perspective, not just its practice (which, in an empirical way – what you saw if you looked out of a window – is to be found in van Eyck), but the mathematical theory which enabled it to be generalized. This made a strong appeal to the Renaissance belief in harmonious proportion based on number, and especially to Florentines predisposed towards a mathematical basis of design by their adroitness with figures. No other city could rival Florence in its knowledge of banking and all educated Florentines were brought up to use the abacus. Perspective, which was unknown to the ancient world as well as to the Middle Ages, provided an accurate basis for the naturalistic representation of the external world and perfectly illustrates how the programme of recovering the antique was compatible with innovation.

Burckhardt in a famous phrase characterized the Italian Renaissance as 'the discovery of the world and of man' – the first, objective in its exploration of the external world; the second, subjective in its exploration of human individuality. The 'return to nature' was a widely-used expression at the time, matching the 'return to antiquity'. Leonardo (1452–1519) described the painter as the 'imitator of all the visible works of nature' and shared the common opinion that the closer a painting was to 'the thing imitated' the better.

The connection between the 'science' of perspective and the representation of nature is an example of a wider interest, characteristic of Renaissance Italy, in the connection between art and science – the latter in the sense of observation combined with the search for a mathematical basis. The supreme example of this is again Leonardo, whom Kenneth Clark described as the 'most relentlessly curious man in history'. His passion to know the how and why of everything he saw filled his famous notebooks, and he insisted that painting, in its pursuit of naturalism, had to be subjugated to the 'mathematical sciences'.

The search for a mathematical theory of human proportions which would satisfy both the Neoplatonist belief in the continuity of harmony between man and nature, and the classical belief in symmetry fascinated

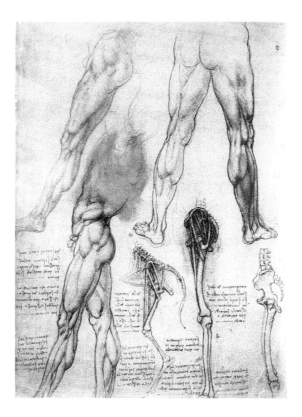

Alberti, Leonardo and Dürer, the last-named always the closest of
northern artists to the Italians. All three wrote studies of human
proportion as well as of perspective, Alberti making it the basis of his
architectural proportions.

Alberti and Leonardo coincide again in the importance they attach to
the artist's study of anatomy and physiology, and there is a long line of
Italian painters who were also practising anatomists, including
Michelangelo (1475–1564) as well as Leonardo. This combination by the
artists of the Italian Renaissance of the observation, description and
representation of nature has been claimed as one of the indispensable
prerequisites for the burst of scientific innovation which begins with the
humanist-scientist Galileo.

In an age when the breach between the arts and sciences had not yet
taken place, this interest in the discovery of the world went naturally
with Burckhardt's second term, 'the discovery of man'. For if there is
one characteristic which stands out from the art of the Italian
Renaissance, it is the psychological power unmatched since classical
times to capture the humanness of men and women. What need is there
to argue in words what can be seen so vividly from the evidence left by a
succession of great artists from Donatello through Raphael to Titian?
This is an image of man which, in all its variety – and one can include the
two artists Dürer (1471–1528) and Holbein (1497–1543), who were

closest to Erasmus, More and the northern humanists – conveys in visual form the humanist belief in the dignity of man. 'Their subject', Kenneth Clark wrote in his last book, *The Art of Humanism*, 'is human beings, grave and passionate, whole-hearted and intelligent.' And like the great Greek artists they portray the 'concrete universal', that combination of general truth with particular experience which, in Aristotle's view, placed poetic and artistic representation above philosophy and history.

Renaissance artists were rarely humanists themselves, but the best known of them in Italy associated with humanists, shared their interests (for example, their passion for the rediscovery of the antique), were influenced by their ideas (for example, the influence of Neoplatonism on Botticelli and Michelangelo), and sought to express them through their own media. Alberti, who stood closest of all the humanists to artists, insisted in his *Della Pittura* that painting was a noble activity, to be seen as a liberal art like poetry and rhetoric. For this reason, he argued, artists must share the education and the company of poets and rhetoricians; art was not to be left to unlettered craftsmen. If this was a controversial view in the fifteenth century, the fame of a Michelangelo, a Raphael or a Titian in the sixteenth, when popes and princes treated them as familiars and the word 'divine' became a commonplace to describe artistic genius, showed how far humanism had changed the status of the artist, at least for the exceptional few.

10

The problems of assimilating classical models (for example, the nude) as well as classical myths and symbols to the Christian tradition were only gradually solved. The fusion of the two traditions was finally accomplished in the extraordinary 'burst of flame and light' (Panofsky's phrase) of the High Renaissance, at the beginning of the sixteenth century, when the masterful Pope Julius II brought to Rome, to work within a few hundred yards of each other, Michelangelo painting the ceiling of the Sistine Chapel; Raphael the murals in the Pope's apartments in the Vatican, the Stanze; Bramante (c.1444–1514) building the new St Peter's and creating the prototype of Renaissance gardens by linking the Vatican and the Villa Belvedere.

This Golden Age, however, ended with the death of Raphael in 1520 and lasted for little more than twenty years. The harmony and balance of the High Renaissance, to which Wölfflin gave the name Classic Art, was followed by a turbulent and troubled period whose artistic reflection is the uneasy exaggeration of Mannerism.

Whether there is a Mannerist style or not, a subject about which art historians differ, there is no doubt about the change between the harmony Michelangelo expressed in the *Pietà*, the *David*, and the *Moses* of his earlier period and the powerful impression of unease created by the

32 Michelangelo's The Creation of Man, from the ceiling of the Sistine Chapel in the Vatican

33 Michelangelo's David. This and the painting of The Creation of Man are supreme expressions of Renaissance humanism

Laurentian Library and the Medici tombs of the 1520s, or the even more dramatic contrast between the nobility of the *Creation of Adam*, which Michelangelo painted on the ceiling of the Sistine Chapel in 1511, and the darkened tormented vision of *The Last Judgment* which he painted on the end wall of the same chapel between 1536 and 1541.

34 Raphael, portrait of Pope Julius II, greatest of Renaissance patrons of art (detail from *The Mass of Bolsena*)

Guicciardini, writing his *History of Italy* at the end of the 1530s, divided the later Renaissance into two strongly contrasted periods. The dividing line was 1494, the year in which the French invaded Italy and the peace and prosperity which had marked the second half of the fifteenth century were succeeded by every sort of affliction and evil. The sack of Rome in 1527 was followed by the siege of Naples and Florence, by famine and plague. Machiavelli (who died in 1527) and Guicciardini (who survived him till 1540) have come in their later writings to see themselves as living in an age of irreversible disasters and have lost the confidence of Alberti and the civic humanists that *Virtù vince Fortuna*, that human courage and reason combined could triumph over adversity. Instead they see a cycle through which all commonwealths pass; and statesmanship can only stave off, it cannot prevent, the onset of corruption and decline. Machiavelli believed this was true even of Republican Rome in antiquity; it was palpably true of contemporary Florence, where the restored republic of 1527 foundered within three years and the Medici recovered their mastery of the city for good.

The last republic left in Italy was Venice, on which Guicciardini and other humanists pinned their hopes – and not without reason, for humanist art at least had still further triumphs to achieve in Venice with Titian (*c.*1488–1576) and the architectural genius of Palladio (1508–80). But the Venetian republic was only able to survive by skilful adjustment to the changing times – and the direction of that change, not just in Italy but throughout Europe, was hostile to humanism. When the violence and intolerance of the Wars of Religion were loosed on Europe and Bruegel painted his frightening *Triumph of Death* (1561–62), the confidence of the earlier humanists in the dignity and creativity of men must have appeared as bitter a mockery of the real state of affairs as in our

35 Brueghel's
Triumph of Death,
painted in 1561–62

own century, when the earlier confidence of eighteenth- and nineteenth-century humanism in the possibility of progress was shattered.

In the sixteenth century, as in the twentieth, the humanist tradition, if it was to survive the disillusionment with the earlier optimism and not to abandon its beliefs to a total pessimism about man, had to come to terms with the insecurity and the tragic element in life which already haunted Machiavelli. One can see the degree of difference if one compares that marvellous but fragile moment of harmony figured in the High Renaissance of the first twenty years of the sixteenth century and the world of Shakespeare's plays, written in the last decade of that century and the first twelve years of the seventeenth. I make no claim that Shakespeare himself (1564–1616) was a humanist. Who knows what he was? The author of a million words, by common consent the greatest of all literary artists, remains as hooded and opaque as if he had never written a line.

But the plays themselves – that is a different matter. Whatever we know or do not know of the author, there has never been a more comprehensive representation of the human condition. As such 'Shakespeare', not the man but the plays he wrote, has a secure and central place in the humanist tradition. As Matthew Arnold wrote:

> *All pains the immortal spirit must endure,*
> *All weakness that impairs, all griefs that bow,*
> *Find their sole voice in that victorious brow.*

There is light and shade in Shakespeare's plays, comedy and bawdy (Falstaff, Bottom, Sir Toby Belch), pastoral and romance (*As You Like It, Twelfth Night, A Midsummer Night's Dream, The Tempest*), but the deepest notes are tragic – Lear, Othello, Antony and Cleopatra, Brutus. No more than Machiavelli does Shakespeare believe that *Virtù* – courage and ambition – can master Fortune. The most men can do is to face their defeat with stoicism. As Edgar says in *King Lear*: 'Men must endure their going hence as their coming hither. Ripeness is all.'

Or, like Cleopatra, confront the ruin of their hopes with a magnificent gesture:

> *. . . Good sirs, take heart;*
> *We'll bury him; and then, what's brave, what's noble,*
> *Let's do it after the high Roman fashion,*
> *And make death proud to take us . . .*
> *Give me my robe, put on my crown; I have*
> *Immortal longings in me. . . .*

Shakespeare too produces his portrait of the humanist prince and it is one which has outlasted all the others:

> *The courtier's, soldier's, scholar's, eye, tongue, sword;*
> *The expectancy and rose of the fair state,*
> *The glass of fashion and the mould of form,*
> *The observed of all observers . . .*

But Hamlet is now 'a noble mind o'erthrown', a disillusioned humanist to whom Shakespeare gives the lines in which he parodies Alberti's and Pico della Mirandola's earlier eulogies and expresses his disgust:

> *What a piece of work is man! how noble in reason! how*
> *infinite in faculties! in form and moving how express and*
> *admirable! in action how like an angel! in apprehension how*
> *like a god! the beauty of the world! the paragon of animals!*
> *and yet, to me, what is this quintessence of dust? Man delights*
> *not me.*

II

The best answer to Hamlet is given by the last of the Renaissance humanists, Michel, Sieur de Montaigne (1533–92). Determined not to become involved in the religious civil wars, which he denounced as 'a true school of treachery, inhumanity and brigandage', he withdrew in 1571 from 'the servitude of the court and of public employment' (the inscription over the entrance to his study) and despite interruptions devoted himself for the next twenty years to writing and constantly adding to the three volumes of *Essais* which brought him fame. Montaigne had a medal struck with the inscription *Que sais-je?* (What do I know?), to which he answered: 'Only one thing with any certainty, Myself.' In his essays, a literary form which he invented, he carried out an extended self-examination, a series of trials or tests, the French word for which, *essais*, gave him his title. In the course of these he observed and recorded his behaviour with an insight that is free not only from self-delusion and the temptation to present himself as better than he is, but also from the equally disfiguring vice of self-hatred and despair.

Montaigne was not interested in the Renaissance fascination with the self as a work of art, of which Burckhardt makes so much, but in self-knowledge as the only reliable key to the human condition. 'Each man', he wrote, 'bears the entire form of man's estate,' and in the mirror which he holds up every man may see himself in all his variability and inconsequence.

The image of man which Montaigne draws owes nothing to the hopes that Florentine humanists had placed in liberty and the civic spirit of a republic – or the desperate remedies which their failure led Machiavelli to seek. It avoids equally the high-flown exaltation of Pico della Mirandola and the Neoplatonists – 'in action how like an angel! in apprehension how like a god!' – or the heroic vision of a Michelangelo.

Yet it is still an image which places man in the centre, if only because everything man knows is drawn from his own experience. The key lies in the watchword Montaigne shared with Goethe – 'Restraint' – a word which he took from the Greek sceptics and which he inscribed in Greek on the reverse side of his medal. It is a dangerous temptation to try to be more than human: man would be both happier and better if he learned to accept himself for what he is. Nor need self-acceptance prove a barrier to self-improvement; it is indeed the condition of it.

Modelling himself upon his master Socrates, Montaigne concludes his final essay *On experience*:

For my part then I love life and cultivate it in the form in which it has pleased God to bestow it on us . . . We seek other conditions because we do not understand the proper use of our own, and go out of ourselves because we do not know what is within us. So it is no good our mounting on stilts, for even on stilts we have to walk with our own legs; and upon the most exalted throne in the world it is still our own rump that we sit on. The finest lives are those which conform to the common and human model . . . with no marvels and no extravagances.

This is the answer to Hamlet's scorn and it is still a humanist answer, its serenity not the reflection of an easy optimism, but wrung out of the bitter experiences Montaigne and his generation had of the mutability of Fortune and a first-hand knowledge of the inhumanity with which men could treat each other.

Montaigne's is certainly an answer but it was a personal one. As anything more than that, humanist attitudes well before the middle of the sixteenth century were out of fashion and out of favour. Luther's nailing of his thesis to the church door at Wittenberg in 1517 marked the end of the extraordinary era of tolerance in the hundred years before. Erasmus the Christian humanist was now condemned by both

36 Shakespeare's plays and sonnets are among the greatest treasures of the humanist tradition

37 On the beams of the ceiling of his study Montaigne had carved quotations from Greek and Latin authors and from the Bible. As an example, the third from the top is a line of Greek from Euripides: 'Who knows if living is what one calls dying and if it is death which is life?'

45

Protestants and Catholics. Luther had denounced his views in *The Bondage of the Will*, published in 1525, declaring that mankind is 'bound, wretched, captive, sick and dead'; that all men's actions proceed from their 'averse and evil' natures. Calvin went even further in repudiating the humanist views he had originally held in favour of the claim that, apart from the elect, the rest of mankind were condemned to eternal damnation. The arts were a particular object of puritan hostility, and an iconoclastic fever of destruction swept across northern Europe. The ideologies of reform, Montaigne wrote, in words the twentieth century can echo, too often coupled 'supercelestial thoughts and subterranean conduct.'

The Catholic Counter Reformation was not content with the revival of the Inquisition and the foundation of such militant orders as the Jesuits, but like the Protestants turned to the secular powers of the state to enforce its ban on freedom of thought. Humanism had dispensed with authority and turned instead for support to the alternative traditions of classical antiquity – including early Christianity. Now authority reasserted itself. Both the Counter Reformation and the Protestant reformers set themselves to suppress the humanist heresy of man's moral freedom and to reverse the emphasis upon man and his activities in this world which had most differentiated classical and Renaissance from medieval society.

38 The final session of the Council of Trent in 1563 marked the end of Catholic humanism and the triumph of the Counter Reformation (painting attributed to Titian)

Naturally individualistic, Renaissance humanism was neither a creed nor a philosophical system; it represented no interest group and made no attempt to organize itself as a movement. It appealed only to the educated classes, a restricted urban or aristocratic, courtly élite; not, as Luther or Knox did – and as the Catholic Church of the Counter Reformation learned to do again – to the broad masses of the uneducated. Considered as an historical force, therefore, it had obvious weaknesses which became plain once those who regarded it as heresy or illusion organized to repress it. But the ideas which it represented, its insistence on the value and centrality of human experience – the dignity of man, to use the original Latin phrase which still has currency today – had far too much power, once they had been recovered and restated, to be suppressed permanently. Difficult though it was to recognize in the late sixteenth century, the future was on their side.

39 The massacre of St Bartholomew's Day (1572) in which all the Huguenots in Paris, some 2,000 in all, were massacred by order of the Catholic Queen Mother, Catherine de Médicis, and the Duc de Guise

Chapter Two

The Enlightenment

I

After the Renaissance, the next step I want to look at in the development of the humanist tradition is the eighteenth-century Enlightenment, with a particular interest in the *philosophes* – not professional philosophers, but described by their historian Peter Gay as 'a loose, informal, wholly unorganised coalition of cultural critics, religious sceptics, and political reformers from Edinburgh to Naples, Paris to Berlin, Boston to Philadelphia.'[1] Paris was its centre as Florence had been for the humanists three centuries before, and French its natural language as Latin had been in the fifteenth century.

These eighteenth-century *philosophes* – to name only the best known, Voltaire, Montesquieu, Diderot, Rousseau, Gibbon and Bentham, Hume and Adam Smith, Franklin and Jefferson, Lessing and Kant – these *philosophes*, like their Renaissance predecessors, carried on an unending debate with each other, were touchy, quarrelsome and recriminatory. But, like the members of a family, to which they compared themselves, they were ready to unite in support of what they had in common, a programme of humanity, secularism, cosmopolitanism and freedom, the right to question and criticize, free from the threat of arbitrary interference by either Church or state.

Never had the educated classes in Europe formed a more cosmopolitan society, with French as the *lingua franca* and frequent travel – the age of the Grand Tour – especially in the first half of the century when wars were less frequent. The publication of newspapers and journals, which first appeared at the end of the seventeenth century, supplemented the circulation of books, and anything of importance published in Paris, London or Amsterdam was immediately translated into the other principal European languages. To take one example, Montesquieu's *De l'Esprit des lois*, published in 1748, appeared in twenty-two French editions by 1751; in Latin in Hungary by the same year; in ten separate English translations by 1773; in Dutch, Polish and Italian in the 1770s, in German in 1789 and Russian in 1801. Voltaire's *Candide* went through eight editions in 1759 alone. There was of course no question of mass circulation – the famous *Encyclopédie* had no more than 4,000 subscribers. It was still a tiny if cosmopolitan élite which the *philosophes* were addressing, but it was a very receptive one, including many of the nobility (not to mention Frederick the Great who would only speak French, and Catherine the Great of Russia) as well as a

40–48 David Hume, Adam Smith, Montesquieu, Herder, Kant, Bentham, Voltaire, Rousseau, Thomas Jefferson

49 A group of
philosophes at dinner:
(1) Voltaire
(2) Condorcet
(4) d'Alembert
(6) Diderot
Contemporary
engraving by Jean
Huber

surprising number of clergy. The Archbishop of Salzburg had busts of
Voltaire and Rousseau in his study, and there were *abbés* to be found in
all the *salons*. Clerics and lawyers, doctors, officials of the royal
administration, as well as the local nobility and richer merchants, made
up the membership of such provincial academies as those of Bordeaux
and Dijon and of the literary and reading societies. The society at Mainz
in the 1770s had 300 members and subscribed to 47 newspapers and 41
French and German periodicals. It was through these, the masonic
lodges, the clubs and coffee houses, that the new ideas percolated down
to the provinces.

In one case at least, that of Scotland, once a kingdom, now reduced to
the province of North Britain, with Edinburgh no longer a capital city
but proudly known as the Athens of the North, the flow of ideas was
reversed. With David Hume and Adam Smith, two of the most original
and acute thinkers of the age; such substantial talents as those of Francis
Hutcheson, Thomas Reid, Lord Kames, Lord Monboddo, John Millar,
William Robertson and Dugald Stewart; with students, many from
America, attracted to the reformed universities of Edinburgh and
Glasgow, and with such debating clubs as the Select Society, all sharing a
deep commitment to the discussion of moral, social and economic issues,
the Scottish Enlightenment could claim to put into circulation as many
ideas as it received.

2

The century and a half which preceded the Enlightenment had seen the
opening up of the tight, closed world of medieval and Renaissance
Europe. The Copernican revolution in astronomy, developed by

Galileo, left the earth and its inhabitants no longer as the centre of the universe, but merely one planet orbiting a local star. If the universe expanded, so did the known limits of the earth itself, with the voyages of exploration and the discovery not only of the American Indian peoples of the New World but also of other historic non-Christian civilizations in China, India and the Islamic world.

The Renaissance had been followed by a powerful revival of dogmatic religion, in a Catholic as well as a Protestant version. The seventeenth century did not lack great individual talents which have their place in the humanist tradition – Cervantes, Rembrandt, Molière – but more important is the fact that it was one of the great religious periods in European history – 'total, imperious and profound', as the French historian Paul Hazard described it. As the century wore on, however, the undercurrents of doubt grew. The outcome of the religious wars was a divided and unreconciled Christendom, and a tendency to carry further the separation of philosophical from theological thought. Descartes (1596–1650) and Spinoza (1632–77) might personally be devout men, but the impact of their reliance upon reason alone in the search for truth was unsettling. Thomas Hobbes (1588–1679), the Machiavelli of philosophy, whose search for security ('Fear and I were born twins', he wrote) reflected the anxieties aroused by the English Civil War, eliminated religion altogether as a source of human values and based morality as well as society solely upon the purely human urge to self-preservation. Traditional beliefs, both religious and secular, were left disturbed by the experience of the seventeenth century. Men were shocked by the scepticism of a Hobbes or a Pierre Bayle, the French Protestant refugee who declared that

50 Edinburgh, 'the Athens of the North' in the age of Hume and Adam Smith

reason destroyed accepted beliefs and even rendered the grounds for doubt itself doubtful; but they did not know how to answer them.

This tide of unease was reversed and replaced by a new mood of optimism in the first half of the eighteenth century. The grounds for such a change of mood had been predicted well before then, in the early years of the seventeenth century, by Francis Bacon (1561–1626) who rejected tradition in all branches of learning and staked everything on an experimental science which would free man from the burden of original sin and restore to him that control over nature which had been lost with the Fall. 'Men have been kept back', he wrote, 'as by a kind of enchantment from progress in the sciences by reverence for antiquity, by the authority of men accounted great in philosophy and thereby general consent.'[2]

There remained but one course, Bacon argued, that 'the entire work of the understanding be commenced afresh' on the basis neither of authority nor (the Cartesian prescription) of reasoning by deduction, but of observation and experiment.[3]

Bacon died in 1626, a propagandist for the possibilities of science in advance of its achievements. But these were not long in coming. The impact of Isaac Newton's genius (he was born sixteen years after Bacon's death, in 1642, and died in 1727) was not far short of Pope's famous epitaph:

> Nature and Nature's laws lay hid in night.
> God said 'Let Newton be!' and all was light.

Not 'all' certainly; but Newton's formulation of the three laws of motion and the universal principle of gravitation not only laid the foundations of classical physics but offered the promise that the same methods would in time uncover what was still unknown. God, it appeared, was a mathematician whose calculations were accessible to human reason, and Nature, instead of being an arbitrary collection of mysterious powers of which man had to live in continual fear, was revealed as a system of intelligible forces.

3

If any man played the same role in relation to the Enlightenment as Petrarch to Renaissance humanism, it was Newton's friend, the Oxford philosopher, John Locke (1632–1704). Locke's *Second Treatise on Civil Government* provided the intellectual justification of the English Revolution of 1688, setting out a contractual view of government as a trust which can be revoked if it fails to provide for the security and liberty of the subject's person and property. Other works of Locke's dealt with education and human irrationality, and provided the classic

51 Portrait of John Locke by Sylvester Brounower, c. 1685

statement of toleration for freedom of thought. But none attracted so much attention as his *Essay Concerning Human Understanding*, published in 1690. Rejecting Descartes' assertion that human ideas were innate, Locke argued that they were derived from our sense impressions, either directly, or else by the reflection of the mind on the evidence provided by them. Locke went on to elaborate the view that moral values, the meaning of good and evil, arose from the sensations of pleasure and pain with which human experience was associated. To the *philosophes* of the Enlightenment, he appeared to have discovered the scientific laws of the human mind as Newton had of the natural world, and thereby opened the way to reconstructing human society on more rational and therefore happier lines. Thanks to the enthusiastic advocacy of Voltaire (1694–1778), Newton's and Locke's ideas – which Voltaire believed were the fruit of the freedom that the English enjoyed – exercised a unique influence in the first phase of the Enlightenment.

Like the Renaissance humanists, the eighteenth-century *philosophes* admired classical antiquity. They no longer felt the excitement of rediscovering a lost continent; having shared a common classical education, they took it for granted, but they identified themselves with pre-Christian Republican Rome. Cicero, with his ideal of *humanitas*, was as much a hero to them as to the Florentines of the Quattrocento. Like the humanists again, they had no patience with abstract philosophical systems, attacking not only Catholic scholasticism but Cartesian rationalism. It was the critical, subversive use of the intellect, not its capacity to build logical systems, which they had in mind when they spoke of Reason; they were empiricists, the philosophers of experience and common sense, not rationalists in the seventeenth-century Cartesian sense of that term. Like the civic humanists of the early Renaissance, they exalted the active over the contemplative life, had no use for

Mon fils, nous demandons nous-mêmes l'aumône,
nous ne la faisons pas.

L'homme au quarante Écus

metaphysics, and were preoccupied with the practical problems – moral, psychological, social – of life here and now. Finally, they shared with the humanists a belief in the harmony of man and nature for which Newton and Locke had now provided an intellectual underpinning. In his *Song for St Cecilia's Day* (1687) Dryden expressed that belief in terms an Alberti, Nicholas of Cusa or Pico della Mirandola would have immediately recognized:

> *From harmony, from heavenly harmony*
> *This universal frame began:*
> *From harmony to harmony,*
> *Through all the compass of the notes it ran,*
> *The diapason closing full in Man.*

These similarities are enough to establish the continuity of a humanist tradition between the Renaissance and the Enlightenment, and the *philosophes* were well aware of this. But they were also aware of the differences – continuity, but not identity. Peter Gay puts it well when he says: 'The dialectic of the Renaissance was ancestor and pre-condition to the dialectic of the Enlightenment; but while the tensions were similar, the resolution was not.'

54

The humanists and artists of the Renaissance had found it possible, in a variety of ways, to combine, or at least to accommodate, classical themes and philosophies with Christian convictions, trust in man and trust in God. 'A wholly secular, wholly disenchanted world view was a relative rarity among Renaissance men of letters . . . the sacred remained a central theme for Renaissance sculptors, architects and painters.'[4]

The tone, the context and the assumptions of the Enlightenment were very different. Accommodation was not enough for the *philosphes*. By the beginning of the eighteenth century, the seventeenth-century revival of religion had lost its impetus, but outside England, especially in the Catholic states, the structures of power which it had created were still in place: in addition to the wealth of the Church, the identification of Church and state, censorship, the persecution of dissent (the Huguenots driven out of France, for example, in 1685), the denial of freedom of thought, the monopoly of education. To the *philosophes* this was the enemy to be destroyed. Voltaire, taking his cue from Cato, the hero of Republican Rome, who ended every speech he made in the Senate with the words, *Delenda est Carthago* – 'Carthage must be destroyed' – ended his letters with the phrase – *Ecrasez l'infâme* – 'Wipe out this infamy.'

The time, they believed, was propitious for an assault on the citadel of orthodoxy. Anti-clerical criticism of the Church for its wealth, its corruption and worldliness could now be supported by a naturalistic view of the cosmos, a triumphant scientific method and the critical, sceptical, empiricist habits of thought which these engendered.

What stood in the way of extending the new ways of thought to the reform of the human condition and human society – a science of man and society – were the fears and inhibitions produced by the mysteries, magic and paradoxes of Revealed Religion which the Church had manipulated to sustain clerical power over man's minds. What was needed was to sweep these away in a programme of demystification. For such a programme the pagan philosophers of the pre-Christian classical world could be enlisted (for example, Lucretius), as well as the empirical methods of natural science, and the criteria of historical investigation. (Gibbon, 1737–94, summed up his masterpiece, *The Decline and Fall of the Roman Empire* in the famous phrase, 'I have described the triumph of barbarism and religion.')

This was a common theme, *the* common theme of the *philosophes*. None outstripped Voltaire with his mastery of every form of argument, from wit and irony to denunciation, in the fifty-year campaign which he waged against the pretensions of Christianity. 'Every sensible man', he wrote, 'every honourable man, must hold the Christian sect in horror.'[5] And in a letter of 1762 Diderot, acknowledging Voltaire's pre-eminence in the battle against error, affectionately saluted him as 'Sublime, honourable and dear "Anti-Christ".'[6] His attack was sharper in the last sixteen years of his life than in his earlier years. 'May the great God who is

53 The frontispiece
and title page of
Voltaire's introduction
to Newton's Natural
Philosophy, 1738

ELÉMENS
DE LA
PHILOSOPHIE
DE NEUTON,
Mis à la portée de tout le monde.
Par Mʳ. DE VOLTAIRE.

A AMSTERDAM,
Chez ETIENNE LEDET & Compagnie.
M. DCC. XXXVIII.

listening to me,' he declared in a volume published in 1762, 'this God who surely cannot have been born of a virgin or have died on the gallows or be eaten in a piece of dough or have inspired these books [the Old Testament] filled with contradictions, madness and horror – may this God, creator of all the worlds, have pity on this sect of Christians who blaspheme him.'[7]

When Voltaire published in 1744 his *Dictionnaire Philosophique* (more than half of which was devoted to religious questions), the governments of Geneva and the Netherlands (both Protestant), as well as of Catholic France and the Holy See, all burnt it and (as Voltaire remarked) would have liked to burn the author as well.

Voltaire's and the other *philosophes'* arguments, however, were directed not in favour of persecuting Christians but of stopping Christians from persecuting others. The most famous episode in Voltaire's career was his one-man campaign to rehabilitate the Huguenot Jean Calas, who was tortured, broken on the wheel and put to death by strangling in 1762 on the false charge of murdering his son to prevent his converting to Catholicism. Voltaire's most passionate plea was for toleration, toleration by Christians of other religions. While there were certainly atheists among the *philosophes* – for example, the Baron d'Holbach – or sceptical agnostics like David Hume, Voltaire himself retained a lifelong belief in a Supreme Being, the Creator of all things. Such a belief, he held, was not discredited but made necessary by Newton's discoveries – a belief with which Newton himself, obsessed

56

with the search for religious even more than scientific truth, would have fervently agreed.

Deism represented Natural as opposed to Revealed Religion, a religion without miracles, priestly hierarchies, ritual, the Fall of Man, original sin, divine saviours, providential history, or religious persecution. This was a compromise originating in England, where the fevers of the seventeenth century had burned out the extremes of religious enthusiasm and left a Church of England willing to come to terms with a 'reasonable' version of the Divine Order. Deism was based on tolerance of all religions. Voltaire's Zadig (in the philosophical tale of that name) ended the theological disputes of the Egyptian, the Hindu, the Confucian, the Aristotelian Greek and the druidical Celt by convincing them that their particular observances were all related to a common divine creator. This was the central theme of another Enlightenment tract, the play by Lessing (1729–81), *Nathan the Wise*: since natural religion was universal it bound the whole of humanity in a moral law common to all. Providence was seen as the agent of a Divine Benevolence in which man shared. No longer regarded as a fallen creature, forced to labour under a burden of sin and guilt, man was held to be endowed with a natural moral instinct of benevolence, while Providence – the hidden hand – ensured that society was maintained by an identity between enlightened self-interest and the common good. To quote Pope once again, this time his *Essay on Man* (1733–34):

> *Thus God and Nature linked the general frame*
> *And bade Self-Love and Social be the same.*

4

Deism was never a popular religion. Even in England where it proved attractive to many of the educated, its failure to satisfy religious feeling is shown by the wide appeal of John Wesley (1703–91) and the Methodists. In Protestant Germany Pietism shows the same concern with 'a religion of the heart'. Outside a few cities, such as London, Paris and Amsterdam, the mass of the population remained attached to traditional religious teaching and practices.

And yet the penetrating power of Enlightenment ideas was such that the majority of Christian apologists adopted a defensive attitude and felt menaced by them, while others – Jesuits as well as latitudinarian English bishops – showed their anxiety to demonstrate that there was no conflict between the truths of Revelation and the new faith in human reason. The expulsion of the Jesuits from France and Spain in the 1760s and their suppression by the Pope in 1773 was primarily due to Catholic governments' dislike of papal authority and clerical intervention in politics; but a secular view of the state and its separation from the

54 The manufacture of soap, one of the many technological illustrations in the *Encyclopédie*

Church was good Enlightenment doctrine and it can hardly have been a coincidence that the Jesuits had been the principal target of the *philosophes'* anti-clerical campaign.

The great discovery of the Enlightenment was the effectiveness of critical reason when applied to authority, tradition and convention, whether in religion, law, government or social custom. To ask questions, to put claims to empirical tests, not to accept what has always been done or said or thought, has become so commonplace a methodology – and we are so conscious of the damage it can do when pursued indiscriminately – that it is hard for us to recognize the novelty and shock of applying such critical methods to archaic institutions and attitudes in the eighteenth century.

For Diderot, for example (1713–84), to challenge the received orthodoxy on any subject was the first step, not to replacing it with a new one, but to opening the mind to fresh possibilities and encouraging speculation. This applied not only to philosophical and religious doctrine or petty conventions of sexual morality but to science as well. In his *Thoughts on the Interpretation of Nature* (1753) he wrote: 'If all beings are in a state of perpetual change, if nature is still at work, . . . all of

58

our natural science becomes as ephemeral as the words in use. What we take for the history of nature is only the very incomplete history of one moment.'[8]

Although he was fascinated by the play of ideas and the elaboration of such hypotheses, Diderot had an equally strong respect for the particularity of facts. 'Facts, of whatever kind', he wrote in the same essay, 'constitute the philosopher's true wealth'.[9] He proved that he meant what he said in the famous *Encyclopédie*, to the editing of which he devoted the best part of twenty years. If it was the *Encyclopédie*'s philosophical and religious articles which attracted the most attention – and led the *Parlement* of Paris to ban it in 1759 – its most original feature was the amount of space Diderot devoted to technology and the care he took to get the details right, as can be seen by the twelve volumes of plates which accompanied the seventeen folio volumes of text.

The intellectual fireworks of a Diderot or a Voltaire should not lead us to underestimate the practical benefits which their efforts produced in the Europe of the *ancien régime*. Greater freedom of speech was only one of these. One can add Montesquieu listing the rights of accused persons; Lessing advocating toleration of Jews; Beccaria and Bentham labouring to humanize a brutal criminal code; Rousseau defending the claims of the child; Voltaire's efforts to rehabilitate the victims of judicial miscarriage; Montesquieu's and Diderot's, Voltaire's and Rousseau's

55 An engraving from Voltaire's *Candide* (1787 edition): 'That is the price of your eating sugar in Europe.'

C'eſt à ce prix que vous mangez du ſucre en Europe.

Candide Chapitre 19.

denunciation of slavery, supported by the Scots economists Miller's and Adam Smith's demonstration that economically slave labour was the most expensive and wasteful of any. These are the beginnings of that series of rational, humanitarian reforms which – despite the pessimism over the results – are among the great achievements of the nineteenth and twentieth centuries.

What made the *philosophes'* use of critical reason so effective was their coupling of it with an equally new-found self-confidence that if men were emancipated from their fears and superstitions (including the false idols of Revealed Religion) they would discover powers in themselves to remould the conditions of human life. 'Man', Bacon had declared, 'is the architect of his Fortune' – another Renaissance theme revived. Freedom of thought and freedom of expression were the conditions of progress; human invention and intelligence the keys, scientific empiricism the most powerful agent. These hopes were qualified by reservations, particularly about the price of progress; but progress, they believed, was possible, if not certain, and the possibility of it rested, not in an inscrutable Divine Grace, or the capricious hands of Fortune, but in man's own hands. Antiquity had taught resignation; Christianity salvation; the *philosophes* taught emancipation – man's moral autonomy,

56 Wonder at the revelations of science: Joseph Wright's painting, *The Orrery* (1766), a mechanical model of the solar system lit by a bright sun in the middle

the courage to rely on himself, the motto which Kant proposed for the Enlightenment in a tag of Horace's: '*Sapere aude: Incipe*' – 'Dare to know – start!'

The *philosophes*' confidence in science was borne out by the progress made in every branch during the eighteenth century and by a series of technical inventions, culminating in James Watt's (1736–1819) invention of the steam engine, on which the Industrial Revolution of the nineteenth century was based. Apart from their more mathematical parts, scientific ideas and experiments were not yet closed to the ordinary educated man by the barriers of specialization. It was the age of the scientific amateur and collector. Voltaire had his own laboratory; Joseph Priestley (1733–1804) who identified oxygen was a Unitarian minister; and scientific societies,[10] as well as a proliferation of scientific journals, allowed the whole educated world – educated in the humanities – to follow the latest scientific discoveries. The split into two cultures had not yet taken place. An illustration of this is the amount of space devoted by the *Encyclopédie*, the bible of the Enlightenment, to science and industry as well as ideas; another the fact that Buffon's *Histoire naturelle*, published in 1749, was one of the century's best sellers.

5

The eighteenth-century *philosophes* were ambitious to do for the study of man and society what Newton had done for the study of nature in the seventeenth century. The formulation of such a project was in itself one of the boldest and most influential of their ideas which became a part of the humanist tradition, and has continued to inspire, tantalize and frustrate successive generations ever since. The Enlightenment's own mixed record of success was prophetic of what was to follow.

The most striking achievement was the foundation of economics, the work of Turgot (1727–81) and the Physiocrats in France, and above all of Adam Smith (1723–90) in Scotland. By the application of critical reason they undermined the traditional orthodoxy of mercantilism. Not only did this lead to economic reforms at the time, based upon the *philosophes*' belief in freedom applied to trade and enterprise; but in *The Wealth of Nations* (1776) Adam Smith went on to construct an analysis of prices, capital and labour, and of the laws of supply and demand, which provided the intellectual framework for the great expansion of trade and industry in the nineteenth century and a model on which all subsequent economists of industrial society have built.

Montesquieu's *De l'Esprit des lois*, which had appeared twenty-eight years before *The Wealth of Nations* (in 1748), has as good a claim to be considered the starting point of modern sociology as Adam Smith's book has of economics. Already, in his essay on the grandeur and decline of the Romans (1734), Montesquieu (1689–1755) had declared: 'It is not

Fortune that governs the world, that is proved in the history of the Romans. . . . There are general causes, either moral or physical, which operate. . . . In a word, the dominant trend carries with it all particular incidents.'[11] In his masterpiece, *De l'Esprit des lois*, he set himself to provide evidence of his belief by carrying out a comparative study of 'climate, religion, laws, maxims of government, the examples of things past, habits, manners' which combine to create 'the general spirit' of a society. Montesquieu was looking for the impersonal forces operating in the life of society – such as the influence of climate and geography – and trying to grasp them in the form of general causes and laws.

This pointed towards a determinist view of society, but Montesquieu was far too conscious of the complexity and variability of human experience to look for any simple answer to the nature of man and society, to draw the network of necessity too tight, or to isolate any particular factor (as Marx was later to do) and assume that it regulated the whole. Moreover, when he came to political systems, the moral imperative of freedom overruled sociological determinism and historical relativism. Montesquieu rejected despotism, however well adapted to a people's physical environment and historical tradition, as inadmissible on moral grounds, even if that involved him in logical inconsistency. There followed the famous analysis of the English constitution which he saw as based upon a separation of powers – an analysis which was to have momentous consequences for the constitution of the United States still relevant over 230 years later.

The *philosophes* had less success with the psychological and moral analysis of human nature than with that of society. There was no subject about which they wrote more, or which they thought more important. 'The science of man', David Hume wrote, 'is the only foundation for the other sciences',[12] and Condillac: 'Our first object, which we should never lose sight of, is the study of the human mind, not in order to discover its nature, but to understand its operations'.[13] Hume agreed, disclaiming any intention of explaining 'the *original* qualities of human nature'. The programme was to be empirical, based upon observation, shunning metaphysical speculation and restraining 'the intemperate desire of searching into causes.'[14] The aim was clear enough; the results less so, producing neither agreement nor conviction. The interest lies in the range of alternatives canvassed – Diderot's materialism; Holbach's determinism; Adam Smith's innate moral sense; Hume's scepticism; Condorcet's confidence in progress; Helvetius' principle of utility – and the objections to them, often explored by the same authors.

Once the authority provided by revealed religion had been abandoned as illusory – and on this at least the *philosophes* were agreed – what basis was there for that distinction between good and evil, between justice and injustice, for the moral, social and aesthetic values and judgments to which they attached so much importance? Was the conclusion to be that, since man is a part of nature, whatever he does is 'natural' and the distinction between virtue and vice, beauty and deformity a purely subjective judgment, on which human beings themselves were frequently not agreed and for which there was no objective validity? Diderot wrote that he longed to believe that 'the eternal will of nature is that good should be preferred to evil, and general to individual good', but elsewhere declared: 'Nature does nothing wrong. Every form, beautiful or ugly, has its cause. Of all living creatures, there is not one which is not as it should be.'[15]

Some were prepared to accept this outright: the atheist d'Holbach (1723–89), and La Mettrie (1709–51), the doctor who wrote *L'Homme Machine*. Others like Diderot could neither dismiss nor resolve the dilemma. It was David Hume (1711–76) who claimed he had found an answer.

Hume is one of the most attractive figures in the history of philosophy, loved and esteemed by his friends, combining benevolence with one of the most acute and sceptical minds of the century, without a trace of that *Angst* which Existentialists and other modern philosophers have associated with doubt. What shocked Hume's contemporaries was his rejection of Christianity, which in his *Dialogues Concerning Natural Religion* he appeared to extend to deism and the argument for design. What has attracted the logical positivists and empiricists of the twentieth century is his rejection of metaphysics and his restriction of knowledge, apart from the formal truths of pure logic and mathematics, to those matters of fact which can be established by observation and experiment. In completing his essay on Hume, A. J. Ayer quotes with approval the famous passage with which Hume himself ended his own *Enquiry Concerning Human Understanding*, published in 1749:

When we run over libraries, persuaded of these principles, what havoc must we make? If we take in our hand any volume; of divinity or school metaphysics, for instance; let us ask, *Does it contain any abstract reasoning concerning quantity or number?* No. *Does it contain any experimental reasoning concerning matter of fact and existence?* No. Commit it then to the flames: for it can contain nothing but sophistry and illusion.[16]

Hume himself appears to have set most store by his writings on morals. He was emphatic that 'the rules of morality are not conclusions of our reason'. But that reflects the restricted role that he assigned to reason, not an indifference to morality. The common identification of the eighteenth century with the Age of Reason is misleading. In this context it could be better applied to the seventeenth than the eighteenth. It was Descartes who wrote a century before Hume: 'There is no soul so weak that it cannot, if well directed, acquire absolute power over its passions.'[17] Unlike Descartes, Hume confined his use of the term reason to the drawing of inferences ('relations of ideas') and the appraisal of truth and falsehood ('matters of fact'); it had nothing to do with the actions, values, motives and feelings with which moral judgments are concerned.[18] Hence, in opposition to Descartes, the celebrated dictum (with which Diderot and other *philosophes* would have agreed, though they might not have put it so flamboyantly as the young Hume) that 'Reason is and ought only to be the slave of the passions, and can never pretend to any other office, than to serve and obey them.'[19] 'People', Diderot declared, 'think they do reason an injury if they say a word in favour of its rivals. Yet it is only the passions, and the grand passions, that can raise the soul to great things.'[20]

But on what then are moral restraint and moral approval or disapproval to be based? For Hume certainly did not mean that men and women should abandon themselves to their passions. He was sceptical not about morality and justice but about the confused theorizing about them.

He found the grounds for which he was seeking not in knowledge but in feeling. Accepting that man's instinctive aim was to increase pleasure or happiness and avoid pain or misery, he argued that this was not limited to himself, that sympathy for others and regard for their happiness were as natural an instinct in human beings as self-love. This was the feature of human nature lying at the basis of all social life and personal happiness. Although (he wrote) it is 'rare to meet with one who loves any single person better than himself', it is equally 'rare to meet with one, in whom all the kind affections, taken together, do not over-balance all the selfish'.[21]

It is from these natural sentiments, not from reason, or revelation, that our approval or condemnation of our own and other people's motives and actions, our appraisal of their being productive of a balance of pleasure or pain, are derived.

Whether this would satisfy philosophical criteria did not trouble Hume any more than in the case of his celebrated explanation of what we mean by cause and effect, i.e. of necessary connection. 'The mind', he wrote, 'is carried by habit upon the appearance of one event, to expect its usual attendant' and it was in 'this connection which we *feel* in the mind, this customary transition of the imagination from one object to its usual attendant' that he discovered 'the sentiment or impression from which we form the idea of power or necessary connection.'[22] All that we have to go on is our past experience of regularity in nature, nothing more. 'All our reasonings concerning matters of fact are deriv'd from nothing but custom; and that belief is more properly an act of the sensitive, than of the cogitative part of our nature.'[23] From which it will be clear that the scepticism for which Hume was famous was directed as much against the pretensions and constraints of abstract rationalizing systems of philosophy as against religion – a humanist tradition that goes back to Socrates.

64

In the last resort, Hume is saying, there is no source for any belief or value – philosophical, religious, moral, scientific, aesthetic – other than human experience and no amount of playing with words will give it an authority independent of that experience. What can of course give support to it is if it is shared by a large number of human beings.

There was a second way in which to provide a basis for a system of values: to found them on the principle of utility, which another Scots philosopher, Francis Hutcheson (1694–1746), identified with the 'greatest happiness of the greatest number'.

This was widely taken up by the *philosophes* in the second half of the eighteenth century. Although Hume did not make 'the greatest happiness of the greatest number' an essential feature of moral approval, he took the argument of utility to be a better foundation for government, law and politics than the fiction of a social contract. In the next generation Bentham (1748–1832) proposed, in his *Introduction to the Principles of Morals and Legislation* (published in 1789, the year the French Revolution broke out), that the test of all legislation and institutions should be whether they maximized the happiness of the greatest number and subsequently turned it into the motive force behind the legal, political and economic reforms for which he and the philosophical radicals campaigned in the first half of the nineteenth century.

It is easy to point out the crudities in Bentham's view of human psychology, not least his 'felicific calculus', the claim to provide a quantifiable version of Hutcheson's 'moral arithmetic'. Nobody did this more effectively than John Stuart Mill in his classic restatement of *Utilitarianism*, published in 1861. But the fact is that utilitarian arguments have become so much the natural form in which the case for institutional or policy changes is put that we easily overlook the novelty and importance of the contribution which the eighteenth-century Enlightenment and Bentham in particular made in formulating them for the first time.

6

There is no danger of that happening in the case of Rousseau (1712–78), who remains as controversial a figure today as he was in his own time. He gave a new and surprising twist to the Enlightenment and the eighteenth-century history of ideas which is of particular interest to our inquiry into the humanist tradition, for, as Peter Gay remarks: 'Occasional diversions apart' – and he has just been stressing his versatility[24] – 'Rousseau's work stands under the sign of civil education, *paideia*.'

I have already made the point that it is a mistake to identify the Enlightenment with the misleading description of the eighteenth

57 A contemporary
representation of the
quarrel between
Voltaire and Rousseau

century as an 'Age of Reason'. There was nothing that would have surprised or shocked Hume or Diderot in Rousseau's claim that it was possible to learn from the emotions, from feelings and the heart, lessons of experience, truths which reason could never establish by intellectual procedures and which provided man with the only sure guide to action. In the second phase of the Enlightenment, after the middle of the eighteenth century, Rousseau's writings stimulated and appealed to an emotional revival, a cult of sensibility, the relationship of which to the belief in critical reason is complex and confusing, but which fills out rather than contradicts the other article of Enlightenment faith, a belief in freedom.

Rousseau was the apostle of this cult, the archetype of the alienated intellectual who railed at a society in which he could not find a place, a difficult, impossible fellow who idolized friendship but could keep no friends, and who began his *Confessions* – for he had a compulsion to exhibit and explain himself – with the characteristic remark: 'I feel my own heart and I know man. I am differently made from any of those I have seen. I dare to believe that I am different from any man who exists.'[25] His life became one long estrangement from his fellow *philosophes*. His relations with Diderot, Voltaire and Hume, with all of

66

whom he had been on terms of friendship, ended in mutual hostility and public recrimination. Yet, as Peter Gay says, Rousseau always remained a member of the family he would not have and that would not have him.

Part of the trouble was his style, brilliant but dangerously ambiguous. His writings, Hume noted, were 'full of extravagance', of ill-considered remarks, of original ideas not thought through, and thus capable of being taken in very different ways. Yet they have an underlying coherence and order in their development which account for the lasting influence he has continued to exert.

Rousseau's moment of illumination occurred as early as 1749 when he came across a subject which the Academy of Dijon proposed for a prize essay: *Has the re-establishment of the sciences and the arts tended to purify or corrupt social morality?* In his later *Confessions* Rousseau wrote with characteristic exaggeration: 'The moment I read these words, I saw a new universe and I became a new man.'[26] He had no doubt of the answer: 'Our souls have been corrupted to the degree that our arts and sciences have advanced towards perfection.'[27] It was civilization itself which brought with it corruption and moral decay: Egypt, Greece, Rome and Byzantium all followed the same pattern.

The second stage in the argument was set out in the *Discourse on the Origins of Inequality* of 1755 in which Rousseau declared that this was the mark of man's corruption by society.

The first man who, having enclosed a piece of land, thought of saying 'This is mine', and found people simple enough to believe him, was the true founder of civic society. How many crimes, wars, murders, miseries and horrors might mankind not have been spared, if someone had pulled up the stakes or filled in the ditch, and shouted to his fellow men: 'Beware of listening to this impostor; you are ruined if you forget that the fruits of the earth are everyone's, and that the soil itself is no one's.'[28]

In his *Discourse on Inequality*, Rousseau depicted primitive man as neither good nor bad, but torpid, superior to the animals only in one respect, his capacity for perfection. But this capacity he cannot take advantage of; he may be happy and innocent, but he cannot realize his potentialities until he passes from the state of nature to the civil state. Rousseau was emphatic that 'human nature does not turn back', and that far from wanting 'to plunge the world into its original barbarism . . . he always insisted on the preservation of existing institutions, arguing that their destruction would only remove the remedies but leave the vices instead, and substitute plunder for corruption.'[29] What was required was not to abandon civilization in favour of a return to nature, but to open men's eyes to the true character of the artificial and corrupt society in which they were living (for which, read eighteenth-century Paris from which Rousseau fled in 1756) and convince them of the need for its fundamental reformation.

58 Monument to
Rousseau as the
reformer of children's
education

Three books which Rousseau published in 1761 and 1762 provided his
answer to the question, What, then, can be done? The first, *La Nouvelle
Héloise*, a novel of the emotions, so far caught the mood of the time that,
in France alone, there were seventy editions between 1761 and 1790; the
second, *Émile*, is arguably the origin of all modern theories of education;
the third was *The Social Contract*.

Man must live according to Nature, this was an old Stoic injunction;
Rousseau's originality lay not just in repeating it, but in linking it to the
idea of human development through education. Rousseau, who
acknowledged a debt to Locke, argued that a child is not an incomplete
adult, but a full human being with his or her own capacities and
limitations. And the key to stimulating children to learn and thereby to
grow was not learning by rote and the parrot-like repetition of
knowledge they did not understand, but the imagination, curiosity and
the exercise of their physical faculties. 'Of all men's faculties', he
declared, 'reason is the one that develops last.' To begin with reason, as
education had traditionally done, is 'to begin at the end'.[30] Childhood is
'the sleep of reason', the time when the senses are keen and the child can
learn through observation – 'Not words, more words, still more words –
but things, things.'[31] If the child was motivated to learn naturally, he
would be eager and have no difficulty when the time came for him to
learn to read and think. Our own disillusionment with some of the
follies of progressive education should not blind us to the revolutionary
and beneficial effects of Rousseau's emancipation of the child.

68

To the question, What is the source of morality, Rousseau answered: Not reason, not the identity of self-interest and the common good nor the principle of utility, but 'the inner voice', the innate sense of justice and virtue which every man bears within himself and which speaks at least as clearly to the peasant as to the intellectual. This inner voice, the voice of conscience, was morally autonomous, it did not depend upon revealed religion, education or any external authority – views which identified Rousseau still with the Enlightenment. His concern was not with the liberation of the emotions, sensibility, as ends in themselves – that would be self-indulgence, and Rousseau, whatever his personal shortcomings (and he was frank enough about these), saw himself as a moralist concerned with moral action, to which he believed the emotions provided the only trustworthy guide. All his writings, he wrote, expounded 'the development of his great principle that nature has made man happy and good but that society depraves him and makes him miserable.'[32] Nothing could have separated him more closely from those who believed in original sin than the heresy of Nature's intention that man should be good.

In his most famous work, *The Social Contract*, Rousseau went further and sought a way of replacing the society which corrupted man with one in which man could at one and the same time continue to enjoy the freedom without which he would lose his humanity *and* accept obedience to the laws without which no society can function.

What was required to square the circle in this way? Rousseau laid down two conditions. The first was that sovereignty must emanate from the people, all of them, and that it must be inalienable from them, they must not surrender it, but continue to exercise it themselves. The second was that, in acting as legislators, they must seek to express the general will, which emerged when men acted with a sense of moral responsibility and considered the common good and not their own private interests.

Plenty of obscurities remained about how to discover and recognize the general will; plenty of doubts about the claim that once it had been given the form of law, all must obey it, there would be no room for dissent and those who refused to obey could be 'forced to be free'. Did Rousseau foresee the sort of despotism to which this opened the door in the French Revolution? Did he ever intend his social contract for a country as large as France, or only for one as small as his native Geneva, Sparta, or early Republican Rome? Whatever the confusion and inconsistencies, however, the fact remains that Rousseau was the first to expound the basic principles of popular sovereignty. The other *philosophes* had looked to enlightened monarchy and distrusted democracy. Rousseau did not, and this was what counted for the future. Nor was it inconsistent with Rousseau's view of human nature, which made the source of moral action not the intelligence of the educated, but

the untutored conscience which was as much the possession of the peasant and the artisan as of the mandarins.

7

In the arts the Enlightenment coincided with the final phase of the age of the Baroque, a style whose once superb authority had been reduced in the first half of the eighteenth century (except in music) to the fragile charm of the Rococo. But the world of Watteau (1684–1721) and Fragonard (1732–1806) had no charms for the *philosophes*: they dismissed Rococo as a courtier's art, artificial, irresponsible and immoral.

Characteristically they expressed their interest in the arts by a critical discussion of their different characteristics and of the traditional canons of taste. The term 'aesthetics' was first used by Alexander Gottlieb Baumgarten as the title of a work published in the 1750s, and the eighteenth-century debate constitutes the opening chapter in the modern history of both art criticism and literary criticism. In this debate for the first time men as familiar with and devoted to the classics as Diderot, Voltaire, Lessing, Montesquieu, Hume, questioned the assumptions inherited from the classical tradition.

Must art serve a didactic purpose and teach a moral lesson – or is its primary function to give pleasure? Is there a hierarchy of subjects suitable for painting, which places historical or mythological subjects above portraits and representative above individualized figures? Are the

scenes from everyday life, which attracted Hogarth and Chardin as they had Dutch painters before them, to be excluded as unworthy of art? Is there any other basis for truth in art than the imitation of nature, 'drawn from the life', or does the successful artist – whether a painter like Raphael, a dramatist like Shakespeare, or an actor like Garrick – create from his imagination acting upon experience something 'truer', more natural, because more concentrated than nature itself?

Are painting and poetry sister arts (the stock tag was Horace's, '*ut pictura poesis*') or, as Lessing argued in his essay on *Laocoön* (1766) and Diderot in his *Salon* of 1767, are there fundamental differences between them, to ignore which does untold harm to both? Is beauty an objective quality, resting upon a musical-mathematical theory of proportion as not only Plato and the Pythagoreans, but Alberti, Leonardo and Dürer had all believed, accepting that beauty is something discovered, not created, by the artist? Or as Voltaire and Montesquieu held, is it something that exists only in the mind and eye of the observer, even if (as Hume added), in practice, the history of taste establishes – empirically, not *a priori* – a consensus that 'the same Homer who pleased at Athens and Rome two thousand years ago, is still admired at Paris and at London. All the changes of climate, government, religion and language have not been able to obscure his glory.'[33]

Besides the critical debate which the Enlightenment inaugurated, its spirit found expression in a contemporary style. If the Neoclassicism of the second half of the eighteenth century and the opening years of the nineteenth could not match the artistic achievement of the masters of Renaissance art, it none the less faithfully represented the ideals of the Enlightenment, both the search for a better world governed by reason and equity, and the desire expressed by Rousseau for a return to greater simplicity and purity. Once again it was to the ancient world that Europe turned for models and inspiration, this time with a much better understanding and knowledge of the Greek originals as well as of their Roman successors.

No one more effectively expressed this than Winckelmann (1717–68), a poor unhappy devil, finally murdered for a few gold coins by a young man whom he had picked up, but consumed all his life with a passion for the ancient Greeks which he had the genius to turn into a masterpiece,

61 Title-page of Winckelmann's *History of the Art of Antiquity*, 1764

The History of the Art of Antiquity, published in 1764. Winckelmann's lasting achievement was to found the history of art by tracing for the first time the rise, development and decline of artistic styles and relating these to the society and culture of which they were an organic part. Such a way of thinking about art and history, another facet of the humanist legacy of the Enlightenment, was a revelation with a future, and led Goethe to call Winckelmann a new Columbus. But what made an even deeper impression on his contemporaries was his claim that the Greeks had immortalized beauty and left a legacy which subsequent ages could do no better than imitate.

Winckelmann's book could not have been published more opportunely. It fell in with and reinforced a revival of interest in the ancient world, already under way, which had an extraordinary impact on eighteenth-century taste and the arts. The revival was powerfully stimulated by such archaeological discoveries as the excavation of Pompeii, Herculaneum and Paestum, of the Baths of Titus in Rome and Hadrian's villa at Tivoli; and by the publication of 'Athenian' Stuart's and Revett's lavishly illustrated *Antiquities of Athens*, Piranesi's (1720–78) engravings of the ruins of Rome. It is reflected in the decorative style of Robert Adam's and James Wyatt's interiors, and in Flaxman's designs for Wedgwood's pottery, produced at the Etruria Works. It extended to the literary cult of Homer, and such other archaic poets as Aeschylus (first translated in the 1770s), Pindar, and the fictitious Ossian; and to the

62 An engraving, published in *Les Ruines de Paestum* (1759), of one of the Greek temples at Paestum, in Southern Italy, rediscovered in the 18th century

63 One of the first Neoclassical buildings, the church of Ste-Geneviève in Paris, begun by J-G Soufflot in 1759, secularized during the French Revolution and dedicated, as the Panthéon, to the memory of great Frenchmen

political cult of Republican Rome, which through the art of David (1748–1825) provided the French Revolution with a classical backdrop.

Architecture was the form on which the classical revival left its most permanent impression. Here was the answer to Rococo, summed up by the Abbé Laugier in his influential *Essai sur l'architecture* of 1753: 'Tenons nous au simple et au naturel.' Beginning with Soufflot's Panthéon in Paris (built between 1755 and 1792), Neoclassicism produced an international style in public buildings which went far beyond imitation and spread from Paris and London as far as St Petersburg, on the one hand, Washington and Virginia on the other. Pevsner describes it as the formal expression of 'the liberal humanism of the educated classes in the early nineteenth century, the spirit of Goethe, i.e., the spirit which created our first museums and art galleries, and our first national theatres, and which is responsible for the re-organisation and the broadening of education.'[34]

8

Neoclassicism, however, cannot be regarded as a successor to Baroque or even to Rococo. By the second half of the eighteenth century, the succession of styles from early Renaissance to late Baroque, which, with much overlapping in time and geographical variations, constituted the central tradition in European art, had come to an end. There were no successors which could match its universality and authority, acclaimed for the last time by Sir Joshua Reynolds (1723–92) in his Discourses to the Royal Academy[35] with the uneasy consciousness that he was defending a tradition which was no longer taken for granted – any more than in religion or philosophy.

As early as the 1770s, a new revolt was gathering force, particularly in Germany. It was directed against the rationalism of the Enlightenment, which was condemned by the young men of the *Sturm und Drang* movement for the crime of subordinating spontaneity of feeling, individuality and the inspiration of genius to the intellectualized rules and artificial taste of a frigid classicism. The identification of this with French cultural hegemony added resentment at the inferiority it had imposed on their country to the anger of these forerunners of Romanticism. But the new mood was not limited to Germany and the young Goethe's novel which epitomized it, *The Sorrows of Young Werther* (1774), ending with Werther's suicide, swept educated Europe off its feet.

Romanticism, however, while it differed from anything expressed before in art and literature, did not represent a unified style. On the contrary, its diversity was the quality which Romantic artists and writers prized most highly as the expression of their individuality, and which has defeated every attempt to define it. Baudelaire said all that can be said

when, comparing it with earlier styles, he wrote that 'Romanticism is precisely situated neither in choice of subject nor in exact truth, but is a way of feeling.'

However indispensable the heuristic device of categorizing and labelling, it can act as more of a trap than usual in a period like the later eighteenth century when traditional distinctions became blurred, and thought as well as art was in a state of flux. It was Diderot's responsiveness to this, his receptivity to new and often contradictory lines of thought at the sacrifice of his own consistency, which was his greatest gift.

Two examples will illustrate what I mean. The first is Neoclassicism. At first sight nothing could be more sharply opposed to Romanticism, yet some of the most characteristic elements in the classical revival can just as easily be described as Romantic – the attraction of the primitive and of simplicity, the appeal to the emotions in painting, the ecstatic language in which Winckelmann wrote about Greece, Piranesi's exaggeration of the scale of Roman ruins, the admiration for the sublime. The cult of Greece was taken up by poets as undeniably Romantic as Keats, Shelley and Hölderlin, and in the nineteenth century the Greek Revival, even in architecture, had become as much a part of the Romantic movement as the Gothic Revival and the enthusiasm for the Middle Ages. Both could be accommodated within the meaning of a word which represents a variety, even a mixture, of styles that the writer or artist may adopt to express his individual 'way of feeling'.

64 Drawing by J. H. Fuseli: *The Artist Moved by the Grandeur of Antique Fragments* (1778–79)

75

My second example is Rousseau. For what could be more characteristic of the Romantic 'way of feeling' than 'the language of the heart', the preference for the simple and spontaneous over the sophisticated, the love and trust of Nature, the revulsion against urban life – of all of which Rousseau was the protagonist, making him as central a figure in the early history of Romanticism as he is in that of the Enlightenment.

More than ever it becomes necessary in trying to trace the humanist tradition to get behind the labels and identify individual thinkers and artists and on occasion, as in the case of Rousseau, to separate those elements in a writer's thought which contribute to the tradition from those which appear to have no place in it.

There are elements in Romanticism, the exaggeration of feeling, the excess of emotion and rejection of reason, which seem to me alien to humanism, but also new insights which enlarge its meaning. My example this time is Johann Gottfried Herder (1744–1803), the Protestant pastor and philosopher, born in East Prussia, who was the most substantial figure in the *Sturm und Drang* movement of the 1770s.

Like Rousseau, Herder was prolific and wide-ranging as well as original in his ideas; equally influential on later European thought; equally difficult, touchy, suspicious, embittered and generally insupportable. Like Rousseau again he has a relationship to both the Enlightenment and Romanticism. He rejected, root and branch, some of the most characteristic Enlightenment beliefs, but accepted others and still needs, even where he breaks away, to be seen in that context. Again like Rousseau, his ideas inspired the pre-Romantics and Romantics, but were also misinterpreted and became distorted in the process. No more than in the case of Rousseau is it easy to apply the word 'humanist' to the man himself, but two at least of his ideas play an important part in the humanist tradition.

The first was already in the air when Herder gave the ironical title to his essay, *Yet Another Philosophy of History* (1774); for it had an independent origin in *La Scienza Nuova* (1725) of Giovanni Battista Vico, who was born in Naples in 1668 and died there the same year that Herder was born, in 1744. Vico, however, like Kierkegaard, had to wait until the twentieth century for his genius to be recognized and, according to Isaiah Berlin, there appears to be no evidence that Herder read Vico's book until twenty years after his own theory of history had been formed.[36]

Herder rebelled against the common Enlightenment view that reality was ordered by universal, timeless laws which the rational methods of scientific inquiry could discover. On the contrary, he argued, every historical period or civilization had a unique character of its own, and the attempt to describe or analyse them in general terms obliterated precisely the crucial differences which gave the object under study its particular identity. Herder was not opposed to the natural sciences; like Goethe, he was fascinated and much influenced by their findings. But he was convinced that false conclusions were drawn from them, and in particular that the methods appropriate to the study of physical nature could not be applied to the very different phenomena of human life and consciousness.

Like Vico, Herder believed that the proper approach to human phenomena was through the historical sciences, including the study of language, law, literature, religious beliefs, myths and symbols as well as institutions, and that the proper subject of the historical sciences was communities and their cultures (in the anthropological sense). Each nation, period, culture, society, was unique in its characteristics. There was no universal ideal, valid for all men – any more than there was a universal, unchanging human nature – but a plurality, with each expressing a particular manifestation of the human spirit between which it was impossible to make judgments of comparative value. To try to explain them by analysis, classification and generalization was to be blinded by the success of the scientific method and to fail to notice that human activities are of a quite different kind, a second realm of knowledge which – unlike natural phenomena – men and women can *grasp from the inside* because they participate in and create them. What was called for was an imaginative sympathy to put oneself in the situation of the human group or society whose activities were to be 'explained', or better 'understood' (the German word is *verstehen*), a gift which Herder showed himself to possess to an extraordinary degree.

This started a line of thought, developed by later thinkers such as Dilthey, Ernst Cassirer, Croce and R. G. Collingwood, which made of history (in the broad sense used by Vico and Herder) the equivalent for humanistic studies – *Geisteswissenschaften* – of science for the study of nature.

And this vision of humanity as living in nations, none of which was intrinsically superior or inferior to the other, each of which had its special and distinctive qualities, Herder extended to the present as well as the past. He saw, as Vico had, the principal vehicle of each *Volk*'s identity and solidarity in language. 'Has a nation anything more precious than the language of its fathers? In it dwell its entire world of tradition, history, religion, principles of existence; its whole heart and soul.'[37] Later, an intolerant and aggressive nationalism debased the idea of the nation, but there was no trace of it in Herder's original vision. Nature (he maintained) creates nations, not states, and as Sir Isaiah Berlin says, 'There is nothing against which Herder thunders more eloquently than imperialism – the crushing of one community by another, the elimination of local cultures trampled under the jackboot of some conqueror.'[38] Nationalism entered the humanist tradition in the generous version of Mazzini (1805–72), whose 'Young Italy' was to live in harmony and sympathy with the 'Youth' of all nations, and in the nineteenth-century Liberals' enthusiasm for the principle of nationality. The cause (as Gladstone put it) of 'peoples rightly struggling to be free' – Greeks, Poles, Italians, Slavs – was later to be extended to Indians and other peoples under colonial rule.

9

Immanuel Kant (1724–1804), last and greatest of the thinkers of the Enlightenment, came, like Herder, from the Protestant north, from the same Baltic province of East Prussia, and never left his native city of Koenigsberg. A man as far removed as possible from him in temperament, Kant none the less considered Rousseau, not Locke or Hume, as the philosopher who deserved to be called the Newton of the moral world, and the only picture in his study was a portrait of Rousseau. There, in the decade of the 1780s, Kant completed the three Critiques – of Pure Reason, of Practical Reason, and of Judgment – which rounded off and brought order into the thought of the Enlightenment, dealing in turn with metaphysics, ethics and aesthetics, and at the same time effecting what Kant himself claimed to be a Copernican revolution in thought by bridging the gap between rationalism and empiricism, for centuries the two principal but hostile traditions of European philosophy.

I do not want to lose myself in a technical discussion of Kant's philosophy. What interests me is that in all three of his Critiques, Kant's focus, like Rousseau's, is on man, not on the transcendental, nor on the natural world, but on human experience, and the creative powers of the human mind and the human imagination. Between the rationalists' reliance on logic in understanding what words like cause and effect mean, and Hume and the empiricists' insistence that in experience all one sees is not cause and effect at all but simply one event following another, Kant interposed a third position. What the connection of cause and effect in itself may be, he argued, we can never know. Kant in effect was taking up Montaigne's answer to the question, What do I know?, and answering (as Montaigne had) that all we can know is what comes to us in human experience – we can never get at whatever reality there may be beyond that. But Kant went on to maintain that what the human mind makes of experience is not random or arbitrary, but follows patterns and categories – cause and effect, time and space – which are built into the human way of seeing the world. 'By means of sense,' Kant says, 'objects are *given* to us and sense alone provides us with perceptions; by means of the understanding objects are *thought* and from it there arise concepts.'[39] This was the bridge between empiricism and rationalism.

Similarly, in the *Critique of Practical Reason*, Kant argued that man was a morally autonomous being whose obligations were self-imposed.

They were derived from his or her intuitive awareness of being under obligation, from a sense of duty, not from the external authority of a religious creed, nor from the external pressures of a material or social environment. Although Kant did not share Rousseau's belief in man's natural goodness, this was the same humanist view Rousseau had taken of the source of morality. Kant was equally clear in his view that while a scientist – for example, a physiologist – naturally looks upon man as a phenomenon like other phenomena, subject to the same laws and regularities as animals or inanimate objects, this is not an approach that makes sense in ethics. When we consider man's moral behaviour, we come up against man's intuitive belief that he is master of his own actions, that he is free.

In another famous phrase Kant maintained that an action is only moral if 'I can also will that my maxim' (i.e., the maxim or rule by which I act) 'should become a universal law' (i.e., binding on everyone).[40] And he used this criterion as a basis for reformulating Rousseau's concept of the general will, thereby finding a way to overcome the conflict between the individual and society.

In the last of his three Critiques, the *Critique on Judgment* (1790), Kant completed his undertaking, twenty years before, to analyse the principles of taste as well as of metaphysics and ethics. Despite the fact – perhaps it should be, because of it – that the range of his own artistic tastes was narrow, he brought order into a confused debate. He was able to do this through his grasp of the character of art – play, 'a purposeless purposiveness', originality expressed through a mastery of craftsmanship, passion guided by reason – and, even more, by his insistence upon the autonomy of art and aesthetic judgments, independent of either morality, psychology, politics or religion.

Where even Hume had hesitated to accept the consequences of his own scepticism, Kant wrote without hesitation: 'The judgment of taste cannot be anything but subjective.'[41] But this did not imply relativism or lead to anarchy. For what men mean when they say that something is beautiful is different from what they mean when they say that something gives them pleasure. The difference is the claim, not to objectivity, but to a universality which rises above personal interest or preference. To say 'This is beautiful' does not state that there is universal agreement; but it *imputes* it, claims that this is something which all men of reason would assent to if once they had fully grasped it. What Kant believed he had done was to find a way of reconciling the evidence of experience that disagreements about art are widespread and fashions in artists and styles change, with the equally certain fact that when men speak of beauty they mean something more than 'This pleases me but may well be anathema to you.'

65 The original of the Declaration of Independence, signed at Philadelphia, 4 July 1776 (detail)

10

While Kant was writing his Critiques, the American Revolution was carried to success, the French Revolution began.

From first to last the *philosophes* had seen their application of critical reason and their advocacy of freedom as aimed at producing practical results. The revolt of the American colonies roused their highest expectations. Even before the War of Independence was won, Turgot wrote that the American people were 'the hope of the human race; they may well become its model.'

There were good grounds for their enthusiasm.

First, the generation of Americans – Jefferson, Adams, Washington, Franklin, Hamilton – who created the United States were heirs of the Enlightenment. During the eighteenth century they had developed their own version and selection of its ideas, adjusting their views of reason, the perfectability of human nature, the moral sense, the argument from design, the inevitability, or at least the possibility, of progress, to their own experience in a new country very different from the historic societies of Europe. There was no greater degree of agreement in America about these issues than in Europe, especially in the latter part of the century. But the questions to be answered, the language in which they were debated, the framework of their thought, even where they differed sharply from each other, were those of the Enlightenment. This anyone may see who reads the Declaration of Independence drafted by Jefferson (1743–1826), with its 'self-evident truths' and 'natural rights of man', and the debates which accompanied the drafting of the American Constitution.

Second, the 'Great Experiment' in freedom and self-government to which they had committed themselves was being carried out in a country which, once it had become independent, was not encumbered by any of the inherited obstacles to reform or progress common to all European countries, a country with no hereditary monarchy or aristocracy, no feudal past, no entrenched state church, no inflexible caste system. When the Americans drew up the constitution by which they proposed to govern themselves, they were as free as men have ever been from the weight of history, or, with a continent to expand into, from the restrictions of geography.

Third, the confidence with which they launched themselves into these uncharted waters (which was part of their Enlightenment heritage) was confirmed by their success. It became an article of faith with many Americans, shared by not a few Europeans,[42] that this could not have happened if it had not been true, as part of the design of Providence, that 'This country [as a Connecticut magazine wrote in 1786] 'is reserved to be the last and greatest theater for the improvement of mankind', the new world in which the *philosophes*' programme came nearer to being realized in practice than anywhere else.

The French Revolution was a different story from the American, not a fresh start in a new country but a shift in the balance of power between classes in one of the longest-established nation states, with a deep-rooted identity and cultural tradition, still capable (as the Napoleonic wars were to show) of dominating Europe.

The part the *philosophes* and their ideas played in bringing about a revolution in France has been the subject of debate for two hundred years. By now, however, the outcome of that debate can be summed up in a few words. The Enlightenment was not primarily a political but an intellectual movement. It sought reforms but not revolution and aimed its arguments at the educated class not the masses, for whom – Rousseau apart – it showed a mixture of disdain and distrust.

Just as the Enlightenment was not primarily political, the origins of the French Revolution were not primarily ideological. The Revolution was the outcome of a combination of factors – economic, financial, political; state bankruptcy, aristocratic revolt, the peasants' grievances, and demand for land.

The critical ideas propagated by the *philosophes*, however, if they were not the cause of the Revolution, were important for two reasons. The first was in undermining the ideological defences and the confidence of the *ancien régime*. It became fashionable, even among the clergy, certainly amongst the aristocracy and the middle class, to be sceptical about all authority, secular as well as religious. The second reason is that when the crisis came to the point of confrontation between the nobility and the Church on the one hand and the Third Estate on the other, the leaders of the latter – the men to whom the Revolution transferred power – were precisely those, the lawyers, the doctors, the journalists, who had been most influenced by the ideas of the Enlightenment. The moderate royalist leader, Mounier, wrote long afterwards: 'It was not the influence of those principles which created the Revolution, it was on the contrary the Revolution which created their influence.'[43] As the confrontation deepened, the radical leaders seized upon phrases and ideas

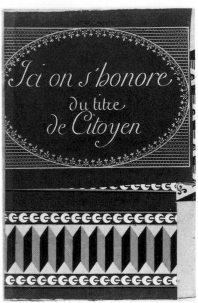

66 The apotheosis of Rousseau during the Revolution: the translation of his remains, surmounted by an effigy, to the Panthéon (see ill. 63), 11 October 1794

67 Revolutionary Paris, a wall-poster of 1790: 'Here the title of Citizen is honoured'

from the Enlightenment and turned them into slogans: 'citizen', 'social contract', 'general will', 'the rights of man', and most powerful of all, 'Liberty, Equality, Fraternity'.

The outbreak of war and the invasion of France in 1792 by the armies of Austria and Prussia, supported by Britain, led to a second and much more bloody revolution. The overthrow of the King was followed by the whipping up of popular support and class hatred, and by the establishment of an organized regime of terror which, in less than two years, led to the condemnation and execution by revolutionary tribunals of some 20,000 men and women, and the killing of another 20,000 in prison.

In the desperate circumstances of 1793–94, the war and the class war became an ideological crusade on both sides, the leading members of the Committee of Public Safety, Robespierre (1758–94) and St Just (1767–94), proclaiming a moral regeneration of France in the name of Rousseau-ist principles and the worship of a Supreme Being in place of Christianity. Those who did not accept the new order – or were even suspected of lack of enthusiasm for it – were liable to arbitrary imprisonment and death, the penalty which Rousseau had proposed in the *Social Contract*, and from which Robespierre and St Just themselves perished.

II

In their anxiety to stamp out the French threat to the social order as they saw it, the opponents of the Revolution took up equally extreme ideological positions. Mallet du Pan, a French refugee who had lost everything but refused to let his judgment be swamped by the infection of fear, wrote in 1796:

There has been formed in Europe a league of fools and fanatics who, if they could, would forbid man the faculty to think or see. The sight of a book makes them shudder; because the Enlightenment has been abused they would exterminate all those they suppose enlightened . . . Persuaded that without men of intelligence there would have been no revolution, they hope to reverse it with imbeciles.[44]

So the Enlightenment ended, as the humanism of the Renaissance had, with a reaction – a counter-revolution in place of the Counter Reformation – which appeared to sweep away all that it had believed in. Even if we accept the *philosophes'* favourable view of the Enlightenment as part of a great drama of which the Renaissance had been the first act, the emancipation of men's minds from the fears, superstitions and false beliefs which held them in thrall, it is clear that they were wrong in supposing their own to be the final act. There is no final act: if the human mind ever is emancipated, it is a battle to be renewed in every generation.

On the other hand, when it *was* renewed after the reaction against the French Revolution had spent its force, it became clear that the Enlightenment had permanently changed the terms of debate, that there was no return to the world into which Voltaire, Adam Smith and Hume, Rousseau, Kant and Herder had been born and which their ideas had helped to transform out of recognition.

68 'The Revolution devours its own children.' The overthrow of the Jacobin leaders and the seizure of Robespierre and St-Just by their opponents in the coup of Thermidor, 27–28 July 1794. They were guillotined on the 28th

69 The Sleep of Reason Produces Monsters, *c.* 1798: Goya's comment on the reaction against the Enlightenment which followed the French Revolution

Chapter Three

The Nineteenth Century:
Rival Versions

I

After twenty years spent in defeating the first French revolution, the supreme object of all the Powers after 1815 was to prevent a second. Never in European history had fear – and hopes – of revolution been more widespread than between 1815 and 1848. Early in 1848 Alexis de Tocqueville (1805–59) told the French Chamber of Deputies: 'We are sleeping on a volcano . . . do you not see that the earth trembles anew? A wind of revolution blows, the storm is on the horizon.'

A few weeks later, in February 1848, revolution broke out in Paris and spread spontaneously right across Europe. Only England and Russia were unaffected. Even when the risings were suppressed, few observers in 1849 would have predicted that 1848 would prove to have been the last general revolution in Europe, at least until the present.

If they had turned their attention from the barricades in Paris and Vienna to what was happening in the back streets of factory towns like Manchester and Bradford, or their continental counterparts, Liège and Lille, they would have discovered another sort of revolution which within twenty-five years of the defeated political revolutions of 1848 was permanently to transform the economy and society of Western Europe and, before the end of the nineteenth century, of a great part of the rest of the world, including the United States and Japan.

There is no need for me to do more than recall the main features of the social transformation which has followed industrialization, changing the whole scale and scope of human history: the growth of population; migration from the countryside to the towns, and from the Old World to the New; the growth of cities; the replacement of an agrarian by an industrial and commercial economy, of feudalism by capitalism; the disruption of traditional patterns of life, first in Western Europe, then – under the impact of imperialism – in the rest of the world; the unification and shrinking of the globe first by trade, then by communications.

In no other period, before or since, has economic growth made so great an impression on those who lived through it as in the twenty-five years between 1848 and 1873 – for three reasons. The first was that nothing like it had ever happened before. The second was that the *rate* of growth, even by later standards, was phenomenal: the world's trade, for example, increased by 260 per cent. The third, and perhaps the most important reason was that the growth, overall, was uninterrupted,

70–78 Schiller, Beethoven, Tocqueville, Wordsworth, Comte, George Eliot, Matthew Arnold, Mill, William Morris

85

79 The first industrial revolution, in the North of England: the railway viaduct at Stockport drawn by A. F. Tait in 1848

80 Declaration of the Rights of Man and the Citizen, decrees passed by the French National Assembly, 20–26 August 1789

creating a widespread confidence that it would continue and open up unlimited prospects of improvement, even for those who had lost out in the earlier round.

The experience of industrialization had a profound effect on the humanist tradition, for the first time confronting an approach which had been developed by élites with the prospect of a mass society, and stimulating its further development by both attraction and repulsion. Once again, de Tocqueville did not miss the double significance of this process. Writing of Manchester as early as 1835, he put it in a couple of sentences:

From this foul drain the greatest stream of human industry flows out to fertilise the whole world; from this filthy sewer pure gold flows. Here humanity attains its most complete development and its most brutish; here civilisation works its miracles and civilised man is turned almost into a savage.[1]

There was little original in the ideas associated with the changes which produced the first industrial society in Britain: all of them derived from the eighteenth-century Enlightenment. What was unprecedented was the force they acquired from being applied in practice and in combination. At their heart was a belief in freedom and the benefits which would flow from liberating human energies from the shackles of

86

DÉCLARATION DES DROITS DE L'HOMME ET DU CITOYEN,

Décretés par l'Assemblée Nationale dans les séances des 20, 21, 23, 24 et 26 août 1789, acceptés par le Roi.

PRÉAMBULE

LES représentans du peuple François, constitués en assemblée nationale, considérant que l'ignorance, l'oubli ou le mépris des droits de l'homme sont les seules causes des malheurs publics et de la corruption des gouvernemens, ont résolu d'exposer, dans une déclaration solemnelle, les droits naturels, inaliénables et sacrés de l'homme; afin que cette déclaration, constamment présente à tous les membres du corps social, leur rappelle sans cesse leurs droits et leurs devoirs; afin que les actes du pouvoir législatif et ceux du pouvoir exécutif, pouvant être à chaque instant comparés avec le but de toute institution politique, en soient plus respectés; afin que les réclamations des citoyens, fondées désormais sur des principes simples et incontestables, tournent toujours au maintien de la constitution et du bonheur de tous.

En conséquence, l'assemblée nationale reconnoit et déclare, en présence et sous les auspices de l'Être suprême, les droits suivans de l'homme et du citoyen.

ARTICLE PREMIER.

Les hommes naissent et demeurent libres et égaux en droits; les distinctions sociales ne peuvent être fondées que sur l'utilité commune.

II

Le but de toute association politique est la conservation des droits naturels et imprescriptibles de l'homme; ces droits sont la liberté, la propriété, la sûreté, et la résistance à l'oppression.

III

Le principe de toute souveraineté réside essentiellement dans la nation, nul corps, nul individu ne peut exercer d'autorité qui n'en émane expressément.

IV

La liberté consiste à pouvoir faire tout ce qui ne nuit pas à autrui. Ainsi, l'exercice des droits naturels de chaque homme, n'a de bornes que celles qui assurent aux autres membres de la société la jouissance de ces mêmes droits; ces bornes ne peuvent être déterminées que par la loi.

V

La loi n'a le droit de défendre que les actions nuisibles à la société. Tout ce qui n'est pas défendu par la loi ne peut être empêché, et nul ne peut être contraint à faire ce qu'elle n'ordonne pas.

VI

La loi est l'expression de la volonté générale; tous les citoyens ont droit de concourir personnellement, ou par leurs représentans, à sa formation; elle doit être la même pour tous, soit qu'elle protege, soit qu'elle punisse. Tous les citoyens étant égaux à ses yeux, sont également admissibles à toutes dignités, places et emplois publics, selon leur capacité, et sans autres distinctions que celles de leurs vertus et de leurs talens.

VII

Nul homme ne peut être accusé, arrêté, ni détenu que dans les cas déterminés par la loi, et selon les formes qu'elle a prescrites. Ceux qui sollicitent, expédient, exécutent ou font exécuter des ordres arbitraires, doivent être punis; mais tout citoyen appelé ou saisi en vertu de la loi, doit obéir à l'instant; il se rend coupable par la résistance.

VIII

La loi doit établir que des peines strictement et évidemment nécessaires, et nul ne peut être puni qu'en vertu d'une loi établie et promulguée antérieurement au délit, et légalement appliquée.

IX

Tout homme étant présumé innocent jusqu'à ce qu'il ait été déclaré coupable, s'il est jugé indispensable de l'arrêter, toute rigueur qui ne seroit pas nécessaire pour s'assurer de sa personne doit être sévèrement réprimée par la loi.

X

Nul ne doit être inquiété pour ses opinions, mêmes religieuses, pourvu que leur manifestation ne trouble pas l'ordre public établi par la loi.

XI

La libre communication des pensées et des opinions est un des droits les plus précieux de l'homme: tout citoyen peut donc parler, écrire, imprimer librement; sauf à répondre de l'abus de cette liberté dans les cas déterminés par la loi.

XII

La garantie des droits de l'homme et du citoyen nécessite une force publique; cette force est donc instituée pour l'avantage de tous, et non pour l'utilité particuliere de ceux à qui elle est confiée.

XIII

Pour l'entretien de la force publique, et pour les dépenses d'administration, une contribution commune est indispensable; elle doit être également répartie entre tous les citoyens, en raison de leurs facultés.

XIV

Les citoyens ont le droit de constater par eux-mêmes ou par leurs représentans, la nécessité de la contribution publique, de la consentir librement, d'en suivre l'emploi, et d'en déterminer la quotité, l'assiette, le recouvrement et la durée.

XV

La société a le droit de demander compte à tout agent public de son administration.

XVI

Toute société, dans laquelle la garantie des droits n'est pas assurée, ni la séparation des pouvoirs déterminée, n'a point de constitution.

XVII

Les propriétés étant un droit inviolable et sacré, nul ne peut en être privé, si ce n'est lorsque la nécessité publique, légalement constatée, l'exige évidemment, et sous la condition d'une juste et préalable indemnité.

AUX REPRÉSENTANS DU PEUPLE FRANÇOIS.

superstition, the dead weight of tradition and the restrictions imposed by government intervention.

Following the example of the Americans, the French National Assembly in 1789 had proclaimed 'the natural and inalienable Rights of Man and the Citizen'. Men, they declared, 'are born and always continue free and equal in their rights', which they defined as liberty, private property, the inviolability of the person and resistance to oppression. All citizens were equal before the law and had the right to participate, directly or indirectly, in legislation; no one was to be arrested without a judicial order; the freedoms of religion and speech were guaranteed. These revolutionary propositions were declared to be the natural rights not of Frenchmen alone but of all men; they were carried through the length and breadth of Europe by the revolutionary and Napoleonic armies. After the twenty years' war the *ancien régime* succeeded in defeating the armies; it could not wipe out the impact of their revolutionary principles. Where necessary, the alternative principle of 'utility' could be used to chop down traditional institutions unable to answer the triumphant questions: Is it rational? Is it useful? Does it contribute to the greatest happiness of the greatest number?

2

Over the course of the hundred years which ended in 1914, representative political institutions and civil rights – equality before the law (although not as yet for women), freedom of opinion and the press, freedom of religion, freedom of association – were established throughout the Western world. More reluctantly and with many misgivings about the perils of democracy and the threat it might represent to property, the franchise was extended, at least to all adult men. These political and legal reforms were only achieved after many battles, from the campaign in the 1830s for Jacksonian democracy in the USA and the Reform Act of 1832 in Britain to the crusade for women's suffrage on the eve of the Great War. A similar struggle had to be waged by the commercial and industrial against the landed interests to establish the principles of free trade and free enterprise. It was the growing success with which these were applied by the British from the 1780s onwards that did more than anything else to validate the general philosophy of rationality plus freedom, of which the political economy of Adam Smith and David Ricardo provided the most impressive example.

The eighteenth-century Enlightenment had staked everything on the belief that if the energies of the individual human being were released, there was no limit to what they might achieve. The extraordinary economic success of the quarter-century 1848–73 appeared to prove them right, to demonstrate that the pursuit of individual self-interest worked for the common good by raising, however unequally, the

standard of living of all – the wealth of nations – and to provide a solid basis, fortified by experience as well as logic, for that belief in progress which has been described as the real religion of the nineteenth century. There appeared to be visible proof on all sides in the 1850s and 1860s that the unfettered exercise of individual talent in a world illuminated by rational calculation could produce unprecedented increases in knowledge and technique, in wealth, welfare and civilization which, given time, could go on to lift mankind to moral as well as material levels higher than anything known before. Progress was seen as natural and, once the obstacles erected by the past had been removed, inevitable.

The disappointment in our own times of the hopes which were raised by the optimism of the mid-nineteenth century can easily lead us to underestimate the scale of achievements, in the creation of wealth and in the development of political and social institutions on which our own Western civilization in the late twentieth century still depends, despite the battering of two world wars, economic depressions, technological innovation, revolution in the developed and rebellion in the

81 The Great Exhibition of 1851 at the Crystal Palace, London

89

underdeveloped countries. It can also easily lead us to underestimate the revolutionary effect, in liberating human energies, such ideas can still have both in the Communist and in the underdeveloped world.

The nineteenth-century entrepreneurs who felt themselves to be remaking the world drew added confidence from the progress of science, which provided the pattern on which the iron laws of economics were modelled. Science had replaced philosophy and challenged religion, providing both intellectual security and the mastery over nature which was the key to technical advancement. Nature and the universe continued to be seen as a harmonious whole, but now in mechanistic terms, freed from the theological reference to a Prime Mover for which Newton had still sought, and explained instead by the First and Second Laws of Thermodynamics.

The demonstration of the superiority of the methods of the physical sciences was provided by Auguste Comte's Positivism, which supplied a paradigm of the advancement of human knowledge through three stages. In the first, the *theological*, phenomena are seen as the result of action by supernatural beings; in the second, the *metaphysical*, these are replaced by abstract forces; in the third, the *scientific*, religion and philosophy become redundant, and positive science produces uniform general laws from which no departure is possible. Comte (1798–1857) was the founder of a positivist sect, the Religion of Humanity, in which the material benefactors of mankind replaced the hierarchy of saints. But his greatest ambition, which he shared with John Stuart Mill (1806–73), was to apply the methods which worked with such effect in the physical sciences to the study of social and moral phenomena. In rival versions both Herbert Spencer (1820–1903) and Karl Marx (1818–83) claimed to have achieved exactly that, a set of deterministic laws, comparable with Newton's laws of motion, which left no room for chance, divine intervention or individual choice.

The publication in 1859 of *The Origin of Species* by Charles Darwin (1809–82) appeared to be decisive in abolishing any line separating the natural sciences from the study of man. There was no doubt – and if there was, it was removed by the publication of his *Descent of Man* in 1871 – that Darwin's view of evolution and the process of natural selection by which it operated, ended the special status of man and brought him within the same biological scheme as the animals and the rest of organic life. In the hands of Darwin's supporters, what had begun as a hypothesis became a dogma. This was one of the consequences of simplifying complicated issues for a mass audience. Popularized as 'the survival of the fittest' and vulgarized as Social Darwinism, Darwin's authority was invoked – by Marx as well as T. H. Huxley (1825–95) – in support of an aggressive secularist ideology, and used to justify a competitive view of human history, the success of the successful, the moral failure of the defeated, the racial superiority of the white races.

I have devoted time to the positivist side of nineteenth-century thought because it is an important phase in the historical development of the humanist tradition and the origin of that version of it known today as secular or scientific humanism. Even at the time, however, the claims of positivism and secularism to represent humanism were challenged by rival versions which saw the nineteenth century and the expansion of industrial society in a different light.

Let me turn first to those who accepted the same revolutionary principles of rationality and freedom, but wanted to carry them further to what they saw as their logical conclusion, and thus complete the aborted revolution of 1789. This led to the quarrel between democratic radicals, who called for universal suffrage, and liberal constitutionalists, who feared the rule of the mob and wanted to limit the franchise to the propertied classes. It was a fight which in the end the radicals won.

The first man to foresee that the demand for equality would prove impossible to resist, and to go on to ask what would be the consequences of democracy, was the young Norman aristocrat Alexis de Tocqueville who set out for the United States to seek the answer in the first truly democratic society. He presented his conclusions in his *Democracy in America*, published in 1835, before he was thirty. De Tocqueville found much that impressed him in the vigour and independence of American life; but he also identified the danger which he believed threatened any democratic society, namely that in order to secure equality men would press for an increase in the centralized power of the state and so, without intending to, would create a new form of despotism. 'They sought to be free in order to make themselves equal; but in proportion as equality was more established by the aid of freedom, freedom itself was thereby rendered more difficult of attainment.'[2]

'The thing itself is new,' de Tocqueville wrote; 'and since I cannot name it, I must attempt to define it.' The danger was that men would become habituated to look for more and more to the state which

Provides for their security, foresees and supplies their necessities, facilitates their pleasures, directs their industry, regulates the descent of property and subdivides their inheritance – what remains but to spare them all the care of thinking and all the trouble of living?[3]

De Tocqueville did not condemn democracy in itself. On the contrary, as he wrote to his friend Eugène Stoffels, he had tried in his account of *Democracy in America* to show that

If democratic government is less favourable than another to some of the finer parts of human nature [he was commenting on the absence of an aristocracy in America] it also has great and noble elements; and that perhaps, after all, it is the will of God to shed a lesser degree of happiness [*un bonheur mediocre*] on the totality of mankind, not to raise the few to the verge of perfection.[4]

To another friend, Henry Reeves, who translated his book into English, he wrote:

I have but one opinion, an enthusiasm for liberty and for the dignity of the human race. I consider all forms of government as . . . means of satisfying this holy and legitimate craving. . . . I came into the world at the end of a long revolution [the French Revolution, beginning in 1789] which, after destroying ancient institutions, created none that could last. When I entered life, aristocracy was dead and democracy was yet unborn. My interest, therefore, could not lead me blindly either to the one or to the other. . . . Balanced between the past and the future, with no natural instinctive attraction towards either, I could without an effort quietly contemplate each side of the question.[5]

De Tocqueville's conclusion was that what mattered was whether a democratic society took active steps to create counterbalances to the threat of despotism by decentralizing power, creating strong forms of local and provincial government with elected officials, independent courts of law, parliamentary inviolability and above all a free press, 'the chiefest democratic instrument of freedom'.

De Tocqueville's own political experience bore out his fears. True to his beliefs, he served as an opposition deputy in parliament and as a member of the *Conseil général de la Manche*. When the French Revolution of 1848, which he had foretold, overthrew the July Monarchy, he accepted office as Foreign Minister of the short-lived Second Republic (1848–52), only to see the government overthrown by

82 On 2 December 1851, Louis Napoleon, President of the 2nd French Republic, carried out a *coup d'état* and appealed to the French people (as in this election poster) for their support in a referendum based on universal suffrage. 7.4 million voted for him; only 640,000 against. This was the decisive step in the creation of the first 'plebiscitary dictatorship', completed when Louis Napoleon declared himself the Emperor Napoleon III in 1852

the *coup d'état* of Louis Napoleon, who as Napoleon III established the first 'plebiscitary dictatorship'. The Second Republic had increased the French electorate from 200,000 to 9 million, but the new voters willingly transferred power to the bearer of a great name who promised all things to all men. Napoleon III's Second Empire (1852–70) thus represented the combination of equality of conditions and despotic power which de Tocqueville most distrusted, and he refused all invitations to serve in its government. Instead he devoted himself, in another classic of political analysis, to showing that the centralized French administration had not been created by the Revolution but under the *ancien régime* which preceded it; and that the French Revolution, instead of overthrowing it, had continued and confirmed it. Regimes might come and go; what remained was the centralized structure of power.[6]

Like John Stuart Mill, de Tocqueville represents that nineteenth-century version of civic humanism which maintained that, in the interests of democracy itself, those who believed in the value of freedom must actively commit themselves to campaigning for adequate safeguards to foster it and check the excessive centralization of power in the egalitarian mass societies of the future. 'Decentralization, like liberty,' he wrote, 'is a thing which leaders promise their people, but which they never give them. To get it and keep it the people must count on their own sole efforts: if they do not care to do so the evil is beyond remedy.'[7]

While the radicals concentrated on the extension of the franchise, the socialists wanted to go further, arguing that political reforms would only touch the surface of the social evils of poverty and exploitation. The revolution begun in 1789 would not be complete so long as there were gross inequalities of property and opportunity, and these would never be eradicated or reduced until the fundamental issue of the unequal distribution of wealth was faced directly. In support of their argument the early socialists pointed, in the name of humanity, to the appalling cost of industrialization in human misery. But their arguments made little progress in face of the conviction that there were 'iron laws' of economics which made it impossible to raise wages above subsistence level, since any gain would be wiped out by the consequent rise in population – as Malthus was believed to have demonstrated in his *Essay on the Principle of Population* (1798).

It was Karl Marx who put the socialist case on a quite different and more substantial footing, by appealing not to arguments based on humanity, justice or morality, which he treated with scorn, but to history. For history, he argued, follows a course which is governed by an 'iron law' of its own, which men can understand and with which they can cooperate (Marx's concept of freedom), but the operation of which they cannot alter. The determining factor in historical development is not men's ideas or beliefs but 'the material transformation of the

83 Karl Marx

economic conditions of production which can be determined with the precision of natural science.'

In the famous passage from his *Critique of Political Economy* (1859) in which this sentence occurs, Marx declared that the economic structure of society was

The real foundation on which legal and political superstructures arise and to which definite forms of social consciousness correspond. The mode of production of material life conditions the general character of the social, political and spiritual processes of life. It is not the consciousness of men that determines their being, but, on the contrary, their social being that determines their consciousness.[8]

Marx's view of history had the advantage of allowing him to show *both* that, at a certain stage in social development, industrial capitalism had a necessary role to play as the one form of production which had the power to break out of the narrow confines of traditional economies and lift societies to levels of productivity undreamed of before – *and* that capitalism must, in turn, as a result of the increasing contradictions inherent in it, lead inevitably to class conflict, revolution, the overthrow of the existing order of society and the birth of a new order in which men would no longer be alienated by the frustrations of inequality and class oppression but free to develop their full humanity.

I cannot myself see that the historical materialism and determinism which are the core of Marxism have any place in the humanist tradition, and Marx himself would have angrily repudiated any such suggestion, rejecting humanism as one more example of the illusions and deception with which men concealed their class interests. As a closed, dogmatic system it seems to me as hostile and alien to the humanist tradition as Calvinism.

But Marx is not as easily disposed of as that, for two reasons. First, as Sir Isaiah Berlin reminds us, even if Marxism as an ideology is rejected and all its conclusions proved false, Marx's 'importance in creating a wholly new attitude to social and historical questions, and so opening new avenues of human knowledge, would be unimpaired.'[9] This intellectual revolution was bound to have a permanent impact on the discussion of man and society, by non-Marxists harly less than by Marxists. It is true that the full effect was felt only after Marx's death in 1883, and that his contemporaries would have been astonished to read such a sentence. But – this is my second reason – they would have been even more astonished, incredulous, if they had been told that in the hundred years after his death, Marxism would emerge as by far the most powerful rival to the humanist and every other tradition, dividing first Europe and then the world as Protestantism divided the Christian world in the religious conflicts of the sixteenth century.

Why this should be so is one of the questions to be answered when we come to discuss what has happened to the humanist tradition in the twentieth century. Before that, however, it is important to look at the other great current of European thought in the nineteenth century which can claim to represent humanist values not, as the radicals and socialists did, by an extension of the rationalist-positivist inheritance from the eighteenth century, but in opposition to it.

4

I have already referred to this when speaking of the pre-Romantic episode and Herder in Germany in the later eighteenth century. 'Germany', of course, is a misleading word. No German state as such existed; the German-speaking peoples were divided among a bewildering number of kingdoms, grand-duchies, duchies, electorates and free cities, and to what extent there was anything approaching a common national sentiment has remained – as it was at the time – a matter of heated dispute. What is not in dispute is that the last thirty years of the eighteenth century and the first thirty of the nineteenth (Beethoven died in 1827, Goethe in 1832) were a remarkable period of creativity in thought and literature, the German equivalent of the earlier Italian Renaissance by which the Germans had only been marginally affected.

Most of the German people still lived in the pre-industrial age, four out of five of them in rural communities in 1815. The largest city, Vienna, had a population of not more than 250,000; Berlin in 1815 had

under 200,000, and the only other city with a population of 100,000 was Hamburg. Many of the best known towns – Weimar, Jena, Halle, Göttingen, were no bigger than those like Padua, Mantua, Ferrara, Urbino, which had played a prominent part in the Renaissance with no more than 10,000 or 20,000 inhabitants.

Like the Italian Renaissance, again, the humanism of this period in the German-speaking lands found expression in an art, the art of music, which achieved the same classical perfection of form between 1770 and 1830 as the visual arts had in Italy in the fifteenth and early sixteenth centuries. Haydn, Mozart, Beethoven and Schubert: for me and for many others the music of these four composers represents as no other experience can the quintessence of humanism, the perfect matching of depth of human feeling with an unequalled power of innovation in the development of new forms.

There is no figure who is more central to the characterization of this period than Goethe (1749–1832). He combined outstanding gifts as a writer and poet (whose lyrics were set to music again and again) with an attitude to life which made him for generations of educated Germans the embodiment of classical humanism. This attitude did not come naturally to him; it had to be fought for, and this deliberate cultivation of an inner balance and harmony gave him a formative influence on the German tradition of education as *Bildung*, self-cultivation.

As a young man Goethe was possessed with that exaggerated, continual fever to which he gave perfect expression in *The Sorrows of Young Werther* – in his own words at the time, 'this violent desire, this violent repulsion, this raging, this rapture' – and which destroyed some of the most gifted of his contemporaries. His account of the stages by which he freed himself from this agitated state of mind to achieve the Olympian serenity of his old age, gives an autobiographical fascination to much of his writing and conversation which eludes us in the case of Shakespeare.

What interests me, however, in trying to characterize the humanist tradition, is not just Goethe's literary achievement, but the fact that this should have been combined with something else. For no experience played so great a role in Goethe's re-formation of his inner self as the discovery of the natural sciences. For fifty years (from 1779) Goethe devoted a great deal of time to the systematic study, in the field or the laboratory, of geology, anatomy, zoology and botany. His original contributions to science were modest but the contribution of science to Goethe's own development – not least as a poet – was enormous. The exploration of the objective world was the discipline he used to curb excessive subjectivity, which he came to regard as the disease of the age. From his biographical studies, he fashioned his own *Naturphilosophie*, metamorphosis, originally the metamorphosis of plants, eventually the process by which the parts of all organisms could be seen to grow out of

85 Goethe's drawing of the inter-maxillary bone. His discovery of this was his most important contribution to science, settling a major controversy about the difference between human and animal anatomy

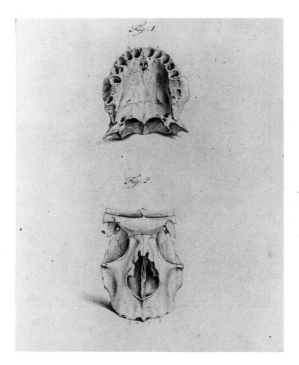

one another. It was this passion to understand the relation of the parts to the whole which led him to distrust the application of mechanical principles to any living thing, the breaking up by analysis of the complete existence on which the identity of organic life depended. *Die Natur verstimmt auf der Folter* – 'Nature is silent when put on the rack.'

To Goethe, as to Leonardo, the scientific impulse, the passion to understand nature, was not separable from the artistic: the laws governing form in nature were the same as those that governed the form of a poem, a piece of music or work of art. 'Man', he wrote in his essay on Winckelmann in 1805, 'can achieve much by using his individual faculties appropriately, he can do extraordinary things when he begins to combine them, but the supreme achievements only come when all his faculties are united.'[10] Again in 1824: 'Man must develop all his human capacities – his senses, his reason, his imagination, his understanding, into a real unity.'[11] He distrusted any of them by itself – the imaginative, or the abstract, or the volitional. The great attraction of the ancient Greeks to Goethe was his belief that they had avoided the unnatural dualism, the splitting up of the human faculties which had settled like a curse upon the modern world. It was this grasp of *die heilsame Einheit*, 'the healing unity', which gave him such a direct power of utterance as a poet and the serenity of outlook which he achieved as an undivided human being.

5

By no means all the German thinkers and writers who were contemporaries of Goethe can be described as humanists. None the less, allowing for the natural difference between highly individualistic and gifted writers – and who could have been more different than Goethe and Schiller (1759–1805), whose friendship between 1794 and Schiller's death is the heart of German humanism? – there is as much common ground between Goethe, Schiller, Humboldt, Schleiermacher, and even Herder as there had been between the Renaissance humanists or the *philosophes* of the Enlightenment. They shared a common belief in the power of ideas to shape life and in the capacity of individuals to develop themselves (*Bildung*) to a point where their inner conflicts would be overcome and they would live in harmony with their fellow men and with nature. This was the ideal expressed in the word *Humanität*, which they believed the ancient Greeks had come closest to realizing. To achieve this was to secure freedom, to rise above circumstances – even in defeat. Schiller in particular believed that the experience of artistic form – in his case, of course, poetry and drama – could serve as nothing else to awaken men and women to their moral nature as the distinguishing characteristic of their humanity – 'Through the morning gate of beauty we enter into the realm of truth'.

The weakness in the German equation of humanism with *Bildung* is that the individual can become so self-absorbed as to neglect that concern with social and political problems which de Tocqueville and Mill, echoing the Greek and Roman view of *humanitas*, saw as a necessary expression of humanism. This was a criticism directed at the time against Goethe for his refusal to identify himself with the German revolt against Napoleon's army and the War of Liberation, and it is one to which we shall have to return in the twentieth century.

It was not a criticism that could be made of Wilhelm von Humboldt (1767–1835), who did more than any other man to institutionalize the concept of *Bildung*. He was born into a Junker family, the elder of two sons, the younger of whom, Alexander (1769–1859), equally imbued with Enlightenment and humanist ideals, became the most famous scientist and explorer of his time, a pioneer in the study of the earth sciences, climatology and ecology. The elder brother Wilhelm, when a young man, spent three years at Jena as an intimate of Schiller and Goethe, before going on to make a brilliant career as the leading Prussian diplomat in the Napoleonic wars and the Vienna peace settlement that followed. True to the humanist tradition which he made the guiding principle of his life, he did not allow his involvement in public affairs and his mastery of European politics to interfere with a range of intellectual interests which extended from classical scholarship to becoming one of the founders of comparative linguistics. But it is the fifteen months which he spent as head of the Prussian department of education in 1809–10 for which he is justly remembered.

86 Wilhelm von Humboldt, diplomat, scholar and humanist, who created the system of Prussian education which lasted from 1809–10 to 1933

99

87 The University of Berlin, founded by Humboldt, was the leading centre of scientific and scholarly research in Germany until the Nazis

In that short space of time, in the middle of the Napoleonic wars when the very future of Prussia was at stake, he carried through a series of reforms establishing the forms of Prussian and German education which lasted until 1933. Following the reform of elementary education on Pestalozzian lines, Humboldt created the humanist *Gymnasium* with its emphasis on the formation of personality, through a *general* education based on the study of Latin, Greek, mathematics and German. As the crown of his educational schemes, Humboldt founded the University of Berlin, with an explicit commitment to scholarly and scientific research which made it the most influential model of higher education in the world until it was destroyed by the Nazis.

Like all institutions, the *Gymnasium* fell short of, and diverged from, Humboldt's conception of it. None the less, the German educational system – including German scientific research which led the world in the nineteenth century as well as the early part of the twentieth – enjoyed greater prestige and, as it seemed to educational reformers like Matthew Arnold, a clear superiority over that of any other country.

Neither Humboldt nor Goethe regarded themselves as more than nominal Christians, and Schiller openly proclaimed himself a pagan. Friedrich Schleiermacher (1768–1834), however, who was almost an exact contemporary of Humboldt's, had an influence on German Protestantism second only to that of Luther. Another accomplished classical scholar, as much at home in Hebrew as in Greek or Latin, he first won attention by his *Speeches on Religion to the Educated among its Detractors*, published in 1799 and followed by a series of *Monologen* or soliloquies. In these he presented a humanist version of religion which derived belief in God not from theological arguments or Christian dogma – man's redemption through Christ's suffering – but from the individual human consciousness, from what Schleiermacher described as the 'sublime hint of the divinity within one, welcome invitation to an immortal life outside the realm of time, and free from its harsh laws.'[12]

With this discovery of the divine working within them, identified as the discovery of men's humanity, comes also the recognition that the way to its unfolding is through the conscious development of a man's or woman's inner life, expressing itself outwardly in their behaviour towards others.

Make manifest your individuality, and mark with your spirit everything that surrounds you; labour at the sacred tasks of humanity, draw friendly spirits to you, but always look into yourself, be aware of what you are doing and in what form your active depths are revealing themselves.[13]

This was the basis of membership of the Church: 'The eternal fellowship of minds, their mutual influence, their reciprocal formation of each other, the noble harmony of freedom.'[14]

Schleiermacher was appointed a pastor in Berlin as well as professor of theology in the new university (1810), and there developed his religious version of humanism as the theology of feeling. Recognized as the founder of modern Protestant theology, he came under attack in the twentieth century from Karl Barth and the 'Word of God' school of theology for substituting a religion based on human culture for the gospel. But they have aroused renewed interest in our own time, and even Barth wrote of him that in any history of modern theology, the foremost name to be considered was and always would be that of Schleiermacher.[15]

6

If we turn to the same generation of Romantic writers in England we find some of the same characteristics as in Germany. Wordsworth and Coleridge, Shelley and Keats shared Goethe's and Schiller's admiration for the Greeks. Shelley (1792–1822) declared, 'We are all Greeks,' and no one ever gave more perfect expression to the impression the Greeks made on him than John Keats (1795–1821) in his *Sonnet on First Looking into Chapman's Homer* and his *Ode on a Grecian Urn*. They attached the same value to individual freedom and to the individual human consciousness as the source of men's knowledge of truth and morality; no poet ever explored it with more perception than Wordsworth in *The Prelude*. There is no comparable preoccupation, however, with something more than the *exploration* of the self, with *self-cultivation* or with that idealist philosophy which was held up to ridicule as high-flown nonsense when Coleridge first tried to introduce the ideas of Kant and Schelling (1775–1854) to English readers – the familiar contrast of German metaphysics and English empiricism which continued into the twentieth century.

88 Joseph Severn:
Shelley at the Baths of
Caracalla writing
'Prometheus Unbound'

One can say the same of the central importance of the historical dimension for nineteenth-century German thinkers as widely divergent as Herder, Hegel and Marx. For this again there is no parallel in England. On the other hand, that other dimension, man's relationship with nature, is one of the great themes of English poetry, which Wordsworth (1770–1850), for instance, unfolded in the *Lines Composed above Tintern Abbey* (1798).

> *For I have learned*
> *To look at nature, not as in the hour*
> *Of thoughtless youth; but hearing oftentimes*
> *The still, sad music of humanity . . .*
> *. . . And I have felt*
> *A presence that disturbs me with the joy*
> *Of elevated thoughts; a sense sublime*
> *Of something far more deeply interfused,*
> *Whose dwelling is the light of setting suns,*
> *And the round ocean and the living air,*
> *And the blue sky, and in the mind of man;*
> *A notion and a spirit, that impels*
> *All thinking things, all objects of all thought,*
> *And rolls through all things. Therefore am I still*
> *A lover of the meadows and the woods,*
> *And mountains; and of all that we behold*

> From this green earth; of all the mighty world
> Of eye and ear, – both what they half create,
> And what perceive; well pleased to recognise
> In nature and the language of the sense,
> The anchor of my purest thoughts, the nurse,
> The guide, the guardian of my heart, and soul
> Of all my moral being.

This appreciation of nature was heightened by the fear that man's relationship to it was under threat. The experience of industrialization did not strike home in Germany until the latter part of the nineteenth century. But already in Goethe's lifetime (he died in 1832) his contemporaries in Britain had to face the disruptive effects on society of an industrialization which has since extended to the rest of the world. The result was to convince the Romantic poets that they could not stand aloof and concentrate on self-cultivation, but that it was their function as writers and poets to express human values which the development of a commercialized industrial society threatened to destroy.

> The world is too much with us; late and soon,
> Getting and spending, we lay waste our powers;
> Little we see in Nature that is ours;
> We have given our hearts away, a sordid boon.

For everything in nature, Wordsworth declares,

> . . . We are out of tune;
> It moves us not – Great God! I'd rather be
> A Pagan suckled in a creed outworn;
> So might I, standing on this pleasant lea,
> Have glimpses that would make me less forlorn;
> Have sight of Proteus rising from the sea;
> Or hear old Triton blow his wreathed horn.[16]

The most original English mind in those remarkable years 1770–1830 was Coleridge, born in 1772, dead in 1834, that shambling, disorganized genius whose range of interests equalled that of Herder, and who combined with it the sensitivity of a great if frustrated poet. Writing in 1838 soon after the death of Coleridge and Bentham, John Stuart Mill described them as 'the two great seminal minds in England in their age'. In Bentham the spirit of eighteenth-century rationalism lived on. Coleridge, on the other hand, Mill said, 'expresses the revolt of the human mind against the philosophy of the eighteenth century', awakening the nineteenth century to all that was undreamed of in the philosophy of its predecessor. 'A philosophy like Bentham's', Mill wrote, '. . . can teach the meaning of organising and regulating the merely *business* part of the social arrangements . . . It will do nothing for the spiritual interests of society; nor does it suffice of itself even for the material interests.'[17]

It was the great merit of Coleridge, and of the Germans whose thought he introduced to England, that they were the first, so Mill said, to go beyond this and produce 'a philosophy of society in the only form in which it is yet possible, that of a philosophy of history . . . a contribution, the largest yet made by any class of thinkers, towards the philosophy of human culture.'[18]

Mill saw this emphasis on what he described as 'the problem of problems . . . the culture of the inward man' as the way to redress the balance and enlarge the utilitarian, rationalist tradition. Coleridge would have agreed with him. Although his own name is identified with the Imagination, he did not believe that the cultivation of this was sufficient by itself to produce the truly educated mind; Imagination must be combined with Method, by which he meant the power to arrange and generalize from experience.

Like Goethe, Coleridge believed in an organic, a holistic view of the mind, of knowledge, and of society, in contrast to a mechanical view. In 1829 the young Carlyle (1795–1881) wrote:

Were we required to characterise this age of ours by any single epithet we should be tempted to call it, above all others, the Mechanical Age . . . The same habit regulates not our modes of action alone but our modes of thought and feeling. Men are grown mechanical in head and in heart as well as in hand.[19]

To overcome this tendency to see men, women and children as parts of an industrial economic system, valued only for their mechanical function, as things, as 'hands', not people, Mill as well as Coleridge recognized the need to pay attention to their human value. In an attack on the exploitation of child labour, Coleridge denounced the *laissez-faire* attitude which regarded poverty and social evils as no more than 'so much superfluous steam ejected by the Escape Pipes and Safety Valves of a self-regulating Machine'.[20] How was this view to be altered? Coleridge had no doubt of the answer: a new kind of society required a recasting of the idea of education on a much more universal basis.

7

To quote his appreciation of Coleridge is an unusual way of introducing John Stuart Mill. From childhood he had been dedicated by his father to acting as the heir of Bentham and carrying into effect the radical-rationalist-utilitarian programme of reform to which Bentham and James Mill devoted their lives. After reading the three volumes of Bentham's *Traité de Législation*, John Stuart Mill wrote in his *Autobiography*,

I had become a different person. The principle of utility . . . gave unity to my conception of things. I now had opinions; a creed, a doctrine, a philosophy . . . the inculcation and diffusion of which could be made the principal outward purpose of a life. And I had a grand conception laid before me of changes to be effected in the condition of mankind through that doctrine.[21]

Mill did not disappoint the hopes placed in him. His *Logic* published in 1843, his *Political Economy* (1848), his *Representative Government* (1861), his *Utilitarianism* (1863), and his championing of Comte and the doctrine of Positivism established his position as the embodiment of philosophical radicalism. Like de Tocqueville, whom he admired, Mill thought it his duty to enter parliament. Once elected, he took up a series of radical causes in the 1860s – parliamentary reform (including proportional representation and votes for women, the latter a cause that earned him great unpopularity); drastic changes in the government of Ireland; a national education act and the abolition of religious tests in the universities – several of which were later put into effect in Gladstone's first ministry (1868–74). His uncompromising integrity won the respect not only of the House of Commons, but of the working-class leaders as well. When there was fear of a serious outbreak of violence in London during the reform bill riots of 1866, and all leave was stopped in the army, Mill was named as one of only three men in the country with the authority to persuade the crowd not to proceed to extremes – and had the courage to exercise it.

But there was another side to Mill, which led him in the deep depression of his early twenties to find his only recourse in Wordsworth's poetry, to declare many times that his spiritual home was ancient Greece (he reread the whole of Plato in the original to write a review of Grote's book on him) and to say of the leading opponent of Benthamite rationalism, 'Few persons have exercised more influence over my thoughts and character than Coleridge has.'[22] What Mill saw and expressed in his essay on Bentham and Coleridge was the need to bring the truths each represented into a common focus, to establish their complementarity. It was impossible to grasp the whole truth of any situation or issue from a single point of view. Hence the sharpness with which he turned against Comte when, prompted by the woman he loved, Harriet Taylor, he realized that in his system of Positivism, 'Comte had lived to plan the completest system of spiritual and temporal despotism which ever yet emanated from a human brain, unless possibly that of Ignatius Loyola.'[23]

It is in his essay *On Liberty*, published in 1859 and inspired, as he insisted, by Harriet Taylor's ideas as much as his own, that Mill brings together the different strands of his thought into 'his constant ideal of human intercourse' (as his biographer calls it), 'an Athenian society tempered by the Socratic frame of mind.'[24] A great deal of the humanist tradition is in that remark.

89 19th-century
technology: the
outsize steam hammer
installed by Krupps in
Essen in 1861

In the permanent debate of Western political theory about the balance between the claims of individuality and the social instinct, Mill argued that liberty was as essential to the health of society as it was to the individual. 'The prospect of the human race is dependent upon the power of original thought, upon the individual rediscovery of old truths and upon the invention of new.'[25] The danger lay in intolerance and the tendency of the majority to enforce uniformity and in the use of the power of the state to secure it.

In the great peroration of his essay *On Liberty*, Mill stated the fundamental truth which he believed no society could ever afford to forget:

The worth of a State, in the long run, is the worth of the individuals composing it; and a State which . . . dwarfs its men, in order that they may be more docile instruments in its hands even for beneficial purposes, will find that with small men no great thing can really be accomplished; and that the perfection of machinery to which it has sacrificed everything, will in the end avail it nothing, for want of the vital power which, in order that the machine might work more smoothly, it has preferred to banish.'[26]

Like de Tocqueville, Mill was not sanguine that his words would be listened to in his own day, but he believed that when men tired of and became disillusioned with the collectivist tide he saw beginning to run, the truths he had tried to state in his essay would have their real value. 'And', he added in his *Autobiography*, 'it is to be feared that they will retain that value a long time.'[27]

106

8

Walking round the great room in the Metropolitan Museum of Art devoted to modern European painting, I have been struck once again by the vivid, palpable image of that predominantly middle-class world created by the French painters of the later nineteenth century – Manet, Degas, Monet, Renoir, an image comparable with that created by Renaissance artists of the Florentine or Venetian society of their day. The same society is held up in the nineteenth-century novel to an even more penetrating observation by a succession of sharp-eyed writers from Dickens and Charlotte Brontë, Thackeray, Balzac and Flaubert to Theodor Fontane and Zola, Henry James and Marcel Proust. The novel, as distinctive a creation of the nineteenth century as the film is of the twentieth, and mirroring in the same way the relationships of human beings with each other, with their families and with their social environment, has as much a place in the humanist tradition for the wealth of evidence it provides of the human condition – what Balzac (1799–1850) called *La comédie humaine* – as Shakespeare's plays had done at the end of the sixteenth century.

Much of the time it is an ugly and discouraging picture which they present – of men and women blinded by illusions; dominated, often destroyed, by their passions; hateful to each other and to themselves; narrow-minded; stupid even in the pursuit of their own interests or absorbed in strange fantasies. But the contrast between the general depressing run of human experience and the heights of self-confidence, endurance, nobility, love, intelligence, sympathy, courage to which human beings can rise is at the heart of the humanist tradition. It would be a shallow and implausible humanism that laid stress on the potentiality of men and women to achieve dignity, goodness or greatness, and ignored the fact that the majority of us are divided creatures who all too rarely live up to what we are capable of. The fourteenth- and fifteenth-century Italians who first spoke with enthusiasm of the dignity and creative powers of man knew as well as anyone the evil, the misery, the poverty of spirit to be found in every street of the cities in which they lived. But they believed that men could rise above their circumstances, could overcome Fortune; that to recognize this was the first step towards doing so and that it was in the possibility of this happening that the recurrent drama and interest of human lives lay. The role the great novelists and dramatists play in the humanist tradition is to remind us vividly both of the contrast and of the possibility.

If I choose George Eliot (the *nom de plume* of Mary Ann Evans, 1819–80) to represent this role, it is partly because of the opportunity it affords to include a woman, partly because her gifts as a novelist were combined with a keen interest in the intellectual and moral issues of her time, on which she wrote for the *Westminster Review*.

Brought up as an evangelical Christian, she went through the characteristic nineteenth-century experience of a loss of faith under the shock of seeing belief in the literal and unique truth of the Bible made untenable by German historical criticism. No one was better informed about the newest developments in French and German thought. She was the first to translate Strauss's *Life of Jesus* and Feuerbach's *Essence of Christianity*, the first (Strauss) summing up the case for a mythical and symbolic in place of a literal interpretation of Early Christianity; the second (Feuerbach) preaching another version of the Religion of Humanity. 'God', Feuerbach wrote, 'was my first thought; Reason my second; Man my third and last.[28]

Feuerbach (1804–72) took the traditional attributes of God – love, wisdom and justice – and argued that the reality was the human potential for these, which men projected on to a mythical God instead of recognizing that the wisdom they attributed to the divine is what men are capable of in their relationships with one another. This remained George Eliot's opinion to the end of her life. In a letter of December 1874 she wrote of

A conclusion without which I could not have cared to write any representation of human life – namely, that the fellowship between man and man which has been the principle of development, social and moral, is not dependent on conceptions of what is not man: and that the idea of God . . . is the ideal of a goodness entirely human (i.e. an exaltation of the human).[29]

But George Eliot was more than an earnest, advanced nineteenth-century intellectual; she also possessed the imaginative sympathies of a great novelist capable of writing *Middlemarch*. These enabled her, in a different way, to do what Mill had been trying to do when he sought to bring together the two main streams of English nineteenth-century thought, the Benthamite rationalist-utilitarian stream which stood outside and tested all received opinions, and the imaginative-Coleridgean which tried to discover from within what was true in them.

It was the second which she made the secret of her art as a novelist. With it she was able to penetrate the power of religious faith and religious experience in other people's lives even when she did not share these herself, for example in the character of the methodist preacher, Dinah Shore, in *Adam Bede*.

In the same year, 1859, that Mill's *Essay on Liberty* and her own *Adam Bede* were published, George Eliot wrote to one of her friends:

If art does not analyse men's sympathies, it does nothing morally . . . Opinions are a poor cement between human souls: and the only effect I ardently long to produce by my writings is that those who read them should be better able to *imagine* and to *feel* the pains and the joys of those who differ from them in everything but the broad fact of being struggling, erring, human creatures.[30]

9

With Matthew Arnold (1822–88) I come to my last group of Victorian critics. Arnold was described by Lionel Trilling in the middle of this century as the man who is 'for our time, in England and America, the great continuator and transmitter of the tradition of humanism'.

Since Lionel Trilling himself belonged to the same tradition, it is worth quoting the definition of humanism which he went on to give:

Let us take it to be the attitude of those men who think it an advantage to live in society, and, at that, in a complex and highly developed society, and who believe that man fulfils his nature and reaches his proper stature in this circumstance. The personal virtues which humanism cherishes are intelligence, amenity and tolerance; the particular courage it asks for is that which is experienced in the support of these virtues. The qualities of intelligence which it chiefly prizes are moderation and flexibility – it wants the mind to be, in the words of Montaigne which Arnold admired, *ondoyant et divers*.[31]

Anyone who reads Arnold must be struck by the contrast between the loneliness and nostalgic sadness which he expresses in his poetry, and the wit and readiness to engage with the most controversial issues of his own day that he expresses in his essays – his description for example of Carlyle as 'a moral desperado' and his classification of English society into Barbarians (the aristocracy), Philistines (the middle class) and Populace. He spoke of himself as

> *Wandering between two worlds, one dead,*
> *The other powerless to be born.*[32]

But his sympathies with the past never weakened his commitment to assisting the birth of the new. He believed that it was the function of literature to act as a criticism of life, to develop in men and women that passion for perfection, 'the impulses towards action, help and beneficence, the desire for removing human error, clearing human confusion, and diminishing human misery, the noble aspiration to leave the world better and happier than we found it', which he regarded as 'the main and pre-eminent part' of culture.[33]

These lines appear in the most famous of his essays, *Culture and Anarchy*, which was published in 1869 at the end of the popular agitation in Britain (the 'anarchy' of the title), which Mill had helped to calm and which produced the extension of the franchise by the Reform Act of 1867. Arnold went on to draw a contrast between 'the mechanical and material civilisation in esteem with us . . . faith in machinery absurdly disproportioned to the end which it is to serve . . . as if machinery had a value in and for itself', and culture, which places human perfection in becoming something rather than in having something, in an inward condition of the mind and spirit, not in an outward set of circumstances . . . in the growth and predominance of our humanity proper, as distinguished from our animality . . . in the expansion of those gifts of thought and feeling which make the peculiar dignity, wealth and happiness of human nature.

Like Goethe, Arnold identified this ideal with the Greeks and the concept of *humanitas* which derived from them and had been elaborated in the humanist tradition. This ideal was particularly important to the civilization of the modern world which 'to a much greater degree than the civilisation of Greece and Rome is mechanical and external and tends constantly to become more so.'[34]

If the tradition was to be continued, Arnold believed that it had to be by converting the middle class which was now the most influential section of English society to the values it represented. From the thirty years he had spent as an inspector of Nonconformist schools he was familiar with the narrow and self-righteous views of the Dissenting sects which he pilloried as a religious version of the prevalent materialist philosophy. The strength of the Puritan tradition, which Arnold did not attempt to deny, lay in the grasp of Hebraism, the principle of morality in conduct, the Nonconformist conscience, to which Gladstone and other liberal leaders appealed as one of the strongest forces in British politics. What the Dissenters lacked, and needed to balance it, was an equal appreciation of culture, that pursuit of perfection which he identified with Hellenism.

Arnold saw the key to this in taking education out of the hands of the churches and setting up a system of state secondary education which would civilize the Philistines and give the middle and working classes access to 'the best that has been thought and known in the world'. He knew far better than his contemporaries how far England lagged behind the Continent in educational provision. In his *Schools and Universities of the Continent* (1868) he spoke with admiration of Humboldt's reforms in Prussia and of the national system of *lycées* which Napoleon, building on the foundations laid by the Revolution, had left to France, together with such powerful institutions of higher education as the *École Normale Supérieure*, the *Polytechnique*, and the other *Grandes Écoles*. It took a hundred years for England to follow suit. Trapped in the sectarian quarrels of Nonconformist, Catholic and Anglican special interests, it was not until 1902 that Morant's act[35] created a national system of secondary education which to this day has still failed to incorporate in it the prestigious schools of the independent sector, a social division for which Britain has paid a heavy price.

Arnold believed that 'moral causes govern the standing and falling of states' and that, as he told an American audience, 'In a democratic community like this, with its newness, its magnitude, its strength, its life

of business, its sheer freedom and equality', the danger lay in the absence of discipline, in hardness and materialism, above all 'from the multitude being in power with no adequate ideal to elevate or guide the multitude.'[36]

90 Education for the masses: Brook Street ragged and industrial school, London 1853

John Ruskin (1819–1900) was as passionate as Arnold in his denunciation of the ugliness of nineteenth-century civilization and its neglect of Beauty. He was prepared to go further than Arnold and argue that this was the result not of a defective education but of the principles on which capitalist society was organized, its one-sided concentration on the production of wealth, its indifference to the production of men. The division of labour was misnamed, he declared. 'It is not strictly speaking the labour that is divided, but the men: – Divided into mere segments of men – broken into small fragments and crumbs of life.'[37] Value, wealth and labour had to be removed from the jurisdiction of the law of supply and demand and related to wholly different, *organic* principles of society which, in *Unto This Last* (1862), he did not hesitate to identify with socialism.

William Morris (1834–96) took Ruskin's argument a step further still:

Apart from the desire to produce beautiful things, the leading passion of my life is hatred of modern civilisation. . . . What shall I say concerning its mastery of and its waste of mechanical power . . . , its stupendous organisation for the misery of life. . . . Was it all to end in a counting house on the top of a cinder-heap . . . the pleasure of the eyes taken from the world and the place of Homer taken by Huxley?[38]

Morris agreed with Ruskin that art could not be revived without a fundamental reform of society, but he had no confidence that this could be achieved by preaching to a dominant middle class incapable of its own regeneration. It required a social revolution and that could only be achieved by winning the working class to understand that they are 'face to face with a false society, themselves the only possible elements of a true society.'[39]

By 1900, the earnest mid-Victorian world of George Eliot and Matthew Arnold was no longer recognizable. Although both Ruskin and Morris were to attract renewed attention in the twentieth century, in late nineteenth-century Britain they were voices crying in the wilderness. Outwardly, Western civilization had never appeared more self-confident than in the last forty years before the war of 1914. The economic subjugation of the world by Western capitalism was followed by its political division between the rival imperial powers and the strident assertion of the white man's superiority. Statistics supported the publicists' claims. But between 1870 and 1900 there had also been a qualitative as well as a quantitative jump, which put the world of the 1900s – a world in which Freud, Einstein, Picasso and Lenin were already preparing the future – closer to the middle of the twentieth than to the middle of the nineteenth century.

The pre-1914 generation had to face something new in human experience, not the prospect but the reality of a mass society created by the growth of population, and shaped by the experience of industrialization, urbanization, and the large-scale organization – whether state, party or business – required to control and manage it. By the 1900s, the extension of the vote and of elementary education gave substance to the prospect of Matthew Arnold's 'Multitude in power', all too evidently manipulable by politicians and by the first of the mass media, the popular press, created to exploit the multitude's tastes and prejudices. Among the latter were an aggressive nationalism and racism and a growing fascination with violence shared by revolutionaries, anarchists and such intellectuals as Nietzsche, Barrès, Sorel and Lenin. These tendencies found plenty of scope for expression in popular support for anti-Semitism, imperial and naval expansion and the colonial wars, the sort of popular culture which the young autodidact Adolf Hitler was absorbing in Vienna and Munich before 1914.

I Humour has been an essential part of the humanist tradition in many forms and every age, from Aristophanes in the 5th century BC to Charlie Chaplin in modern times. It is represented here by a 4th-century BC Greek vase showing a farce being performed by a dancing girl and two clowns in front of Dionysus, the god of ecstasy and revels.

II Federigo da Montefeltro and his young son Guidobaldo attending a discourse by a humanist scholar (probably Paul of Middlebourg), in Federigo's palace of Urbino. Educated at the Mantuan school of Vittorino da Feltre, Federigo laid the foundation of his fortunes as a condottiere, but was devoted to, and skilled in, scholarship and the arts, and made the court of his poor, mountainous duchy into a brilliant centre of Renaissance humanism.

III A painted panel made for a Florentine
marriage chest (*cassone*) in the 15th century.
Famous Florentine artists such as Botticelli,
Paolo Uccello and Donatello were employed to
decorate such panels, and classical themes were
frequently chosen – in this case the triumphal
entry of the Emperor Vespasian and his son
Titus into Rome in AD 70.

IV The first page of Ficino's translation of the
Enneads of the Egyptian Neoplatonist
philosopher Plotinus (AD 204–70) dedicated to
Lorenzo de Medici. Plotinus' Greek text was
recovered in the 15th century and Ficino, who
had already translated Plato's dialogues into
Latin for Cosimo de Medici, was commissioned
by Cosimo's grandson Lorenzo to make a
Latin translation of Plato's most important
interpreter.

V Holbein's *The French Ambassadors*, Jean de Dinteville and Georges de Selve, painted in London in 1533. The objects on the stand represent characteristic humanist interests in geography, mathematics, astronomy and music. In the foreground is a distorted death's head, which is said to be both a reminder of man's mortality and a pun on Holbein's own name meaning 'skull'.

VI–VII The individual portrait – including the artist's self-portrait – was one of the distinctive contributions of the Renaissance to the humanist tradition. VI: Erasmus was painted by both Dürer and Holbein; the figure of St Luke in King's College Chapel has long been thought to be a portrait of him as he appeared in his Cambridge years, 1511–14. VII: Raphael's portrait of a Florentine patron of the arts, Angelo Doni.

VIII–IX Dürer's self-portrait of 1500 in the guise of Christ: 'It states, not what the artist claims to be, but what he must humbly endeavour to become: a man entrusted with a gift which implies both the tragedy and the triumph of the "Eritis sicut Deus"' (Panofsky). In the 17th century, Rembrandt painted an unequalled series of self-portraits. This one dates from the later 1650s.

X Portrait of Diderot by Fragonard. Best known at the time as the editor of the *Encyclopédie*, Denis Diderot (1713–1784) appears to many modern critics to be the most original mind of the French Enlightenment, the archetype of the French intellectual who made contributions to philosophy, psychology and ethics; to dramatic and aesthetic theory; to literary criticism and fiction (his novel *Le Neveu de Rameau* deeply impressed both Goethe and Freud); to scientific speculation and politics.

XI The design and embellishment of gardens represents another humanist art which dates from the Renaissance. In the 20th century this provides an example of a form of expression designed for the pleasure of a social élite which has been successfully adapted for the cultivation and enjoyment by millions drawn from all classes. Stourhead, perhaps the finest of English 18th-century gardens, was laid out in the early 1740s for the banker Henry Hoare who assembled all the elements of the classical landscape described by Vergil and set these off with 'architectural incidents', of which Henry Flitcroft's Neoclassical Pantheon, seen across the lake, is the most substantial.

XII A cabinet of scientific curiosities, painted by Jacques de Lajoue in 1734, as an overdoor for the collection of shells and other specimens, architectural and engineering models, and scientific instruments, made by Joseph Bonnier de la Mosson and housed in the Hotel du Lude, Paris. Such collections were fashionable in the 18th century and Lajoue's design picks up many of the features in one of the best known of them.

XIII Hogarth's portrait of his servants, painted in the 1750s. A rebel against the Grand Manner (see p. 74) and 'what the puffers in books call "the great style of history painting"', Hogarth delighted to take his subjects from the everyday life and characters of his own time, letting their humanity speak for itself without embellishment.

XIV The birth of a new nation. The American Declaration of Independence (July 1776) was the first formal statement by a representative body of the right of a people to a government of their own choosing. John Trumbull's painting shows the moment when the drafting committee led by Jefferson (with Franklin on his left) presented the document to the Continental Congress of the United States.

XV An allegory of the French Revolution by Jeaurat de Bertry. Rousseau is shown as the Revolution's spiritual father, presiding over the eye of Truth and the tricolour, an obelisk to Equality, a monument to the revolutionary virtues (the rods and axe of the fasces, in imitation of Republican Rome, topped by a *bonnet rouge*), the Tree of Liberty and two half-built columns of 'Regeneration'.

XVI Portrait of Goethe in the Campagna painted by J. H. W. Tischbein during the Italian journey of 1786–88, the turning point in the development of Goethe's genius when he was in his late thirties.

XVII Portrait of Coleridge at the age of 32 painted by James Northcote in 1804. Mill described Coleridge as one of the two seminal minds of his time (see p. 103), a view confirmed in the 20th century not only by renewed appreciation of his poetry but also by the recovery of the full range of his critical and philosophical thinking.

XVIII *Morning amongst the Coniston Fells* in the Lake District, one of Turner's early landscapes exhibited in 1798, the year in which Wordsworth and Coleridge published their *Lyrical Ballads*. The greatest of all landscape painters, according to Ruskin, Turner illustrates the fascination of the artists and writers of the Romantic period with Man's response to Nature.

XIX Greece's struggle for liberation from
Turkish rule, with its unique combination of
classical, Romantic and nationalist associations,
roused great enthusiasm in Western Europe.
Byron died trying to organize an army at
Missolonghi in 1824, and when the town was
eventually taken, Delacroix painted this allegory
Greece expiring on the ruins of Missolonghi.

XX 1848 became known as the Year of
Revolutions. Beginning in Sicily, the
revolutionary ferment, which combined social
discontent with political demands, spread
throughout Europe. In Paris, Louis Philippe
abdicated in February, but the republican
government which took his place had to face a
workers' revolt in the 'June Days'. N. E. Gabé's
painting depicts an attack by the Paris
revolutionaries on the Panthéon on 21 June,
before the revolt was suppressed by force.

XXI *Réunion de Famille*, painted by Frédéric Bazille in 1867, characterizes the bourgeois family which was the central institution of 19th-century middle-class European society and the target of every avant-garde writer and revolutionary. Bazille (1841–70) was a friend of Renoir, Monet and Manet. A painter of great promise, he was killed in action in the Franco-Prussian war before he was thirty.

Four answers to the question, Has modern art a place in the humanist tradition?

XXII Paul Klee's delicate world of fantasy and wit: *A Young Lady's Adventure* (1922).

XXIII Matisse's mastery of colour: *Tristesse du Roi*, a gouache inspired by the Biblical theme of King David in *The Song of Songs*. By 1952, when this was created, Matisse was in his eighties, ill, confined to bed and unable to paint; but he could still cut shapes out of coloured paper and arrange them to form patterns. He described this as 'drawing with scissors', a final burst of innovative energy in defiance of physical handicap.

XXIV One of Picasso's *Las Meninas* (1957), a
series of variations on a traditional theme, in
this case Velasquez's painting of 1656 with the
same title. Picasso greatly admired Velasquez's
picture and used it as the starting point for a
whole range of surrealist images and associations
which it suggested to him, exploring and
expanding the original without ever losing
touch with it.

XXV *Two forms (Divided Circle)*, a bronze by
Barbara Hepworth. Her sculpture was deeply
influenced by the shapes she found in nature,
and she underlined the connection by placing
this and more than twenty other pieces in the
garden she created at her home in St Ives. See
note 21 on pp. 202–03.

XXVI Arne Jacobsen's design for
St Catherine's College, Oxford,
opened in 1964, and notable for
the combination of modern forms
with the human scale and
traditional features of an Oxford
college. For Pevsner's comment,
see note 21 on pp. 202–03.

XXVII New York, as generations
of immigrants have seen it from
the sea. No other city's skyline so
powerfully epitomizes the 20th
century in its Promethean
achievement, and its human
suffering.

Where was the humanist tradition to be found in this new world?

One obvious answer is the key role liberalism had played in creating it. For example, the statistics I spoke of showed a substantial growth of industry, trade and wealth on a scale and for a longer period than anything experienced, or even conceived of, before. There were fluctuations, but overall between 1870 and 1900 world industrial production increased nearly four times; in the thirty years after the mid-'70s the volume of world trade trebled; between 1898 and 1913 alone its value doubled. Free trade no longer passed unchallenged; there was a strong reaction in favour of protectionism. This did not detract, however, from the part played in releasing the human energies on which the achievement was based by the economic liberalism first formulated by Adam Smith, restated by John Stuart Mill and given its final form by Alfred Marshall in 1890.[40]

Material had been matched by political progress. By the end of the nineteenth century constitutional government and parliamentary institutions had been established throughout the Western world, with the continued extension of a more democratic franchise. The unification of Germany and Italy, the creation of new states in the Balkans at the expense of the Turkish Empire, the concessions which the Dual Monarchy was forced to make to its subject nationalities, represented so many triumphs for the principle of nationality. Similar gains had been won by liberal parties in their campaign to secularize the state and laicize education – culminating, in France, in the radicals' success in the Dreyfus Affair, the expulsion of the Jesuits and other teaching orders, and the law of 1905 separating church and state.

Taken together, these achievements are enough to justify the common description of the years 1870–1914 as the zenith of liberalism, to which the humanist tradition had contributed so much. But the term 'zenith' also implies that, having reached its peak, liberalism had lost its growing power and impetus. A sign of this was the divisions and hesitation of liberal parties in face of such new problems as protectionism, socialism and imperialism. The same was true of liberal ideas. Widely diffused, they had come to be taken for granted by those who held them, had lost their originality and stiffened into orthodoxy, with little appeal any longer to a new generation.

This is what had also happened to the rationalist-utilitarian-positivist tradition which claimed, via Bentham, the philosophical radicals and Comte, to be the heir of the Enlightenment. It still stood high in public estimation, buttressed on the one side by the successes of natural science and on the other by the unchallenged 'laws' of political economy. Drawing his inspiration from Darwin, Herbert Spencer had devoted his lifetime (he completed the ten volumes of his *Synthetic Philosophy* in 1896) to elaborating the grounds for confidence in rational progress and the universal validity of the scientific method which sustained it. Karl

Pearson, one of the founders of modern statistics (1857–1936), proclaimed: 'The whole range of phenomena, mental as well as biological – the entire universe – is its field. The scientific method is the sole gateway to the whole region of knowledge.'[41] Hippolyte Taine (1828–93) undertook to show how it could be applied to the cultural field, in the study of literature, art and philosophy, claiming that these were social products, owing little to individual talent or volition, far more to a combination of such impersonal conditioning factors as '*la race*', a writer's physical and psychological inheritance; '*le milieu*', his geographical, social and political environment; and '*le moment*', the historical situation in which he found himself.

In the final year of the nineteenth century Ernst Haeckel (1834–1919) published *The Riddle of the Universe*, one of the most successful works of scientific popularization ever marketed, which sold hundreds of thousands of copies throughout the Western world. This summed up the positivist view in what Haeckel described as 'a rounded philosophical system', providing a solution of the enigmas which had perplexed mankind since the Greeks. In 1906 he characterized his 'monist' philosophy as the belief that

a vast, uniform, uninterrupted and eternal process of development obtains throughout all nature; and that all natural phenomena without exception, from the motion of the heavenly bodies and the fall of a rolling stone to the growth of plants and the consciousness of men, obey one and the same great law of causation; that all may be ultimately referred to the mechanics of atoms.[42]

This positivist faith in science, and the belief in progress which it sustained, had moved a long way from that critical open-ended use of reason by a Diderot or a Hume. Having broken the monopoly which religion and the Church held over men's minds, rationalism had in its turn become a dogmatic ideology, equally closed to examination of its assumptions and hardly less intolerant of dissent. It was this intolerance which led Mill to turn against it as a system of despotism.[43]

I have no more sympathy than Mill with the claim of nineteenth-century positivism to represent the humanist tradition. But I see that it has to be included in any account of that tradition, for two reasons. The first is the confidence in the future which it engendered. If there is one point on which observers of the late nineteenth–early twentieth century agree, it is that this was the most important feature which distinguished the pre-war from the post-war world. Had it been possible to hold an opinion poll in the industrialized countries in the 1900s, it is a fair guess that a majority would have expressed their belief in the continued material and social progress of mankind – so strong was the spell still cast over men's minds by the extraordinary expansion of the economy, the transformation of a rural into an increasingly urban society, the extension of the white races' supremacy over the whole world, and the limitless prospects opened up by the application of science to the mastery of nature.

The second and very different reason is the *vulnerability* of the belief in progress and the consequences for the humanist tradition of its collapse under the combined impact of the First World War, the Depression of the 1930s and the rise of Fascism. For when that happened not only was all confidence in progress lost, but in the bitterness of their disillusionment many repudiated liberalism and its humanist origins *en bloc* for having first encouraged and then cheated the hopes they had built on them.

My question then has to be put differently. Now that we know what lay ahead after 1914, can we detect any signs before that date of the humanist tradition developing in new directions which would enable it to survive the decline of liberalism?

Chapter Four

The Twentieth Century:
Towards a New Humanism

I

I shall never forget the intellectual excitement of discovering that the transition in Western civilization from the nineteenth to the twentieth century began, not, as I had grown up believing, with the outbreak of war in 1914, but before that, in the late nineteenth century and the earlier years of the twentieth.[1]

A good starting-point is 1883, the year in which the Danish critic Georg Brandes (1842–1927) published a volume of essays with the title *Men of the Modern Breakthrough*. Brandes's use of the word 'modern' immediately caught on. It became a rallying cry in a fierce debate in Germany, Northern and Central Europe – What is the meaning of 'modern'? For or against? – which lasted from the 1880s to the 1900s. In Paris, London and New York, the 'modern period' begins later. With splendid exaggeration, Virginia Woolf (1882–1941) wrote:

On or about December 1910, human nature changed . . . All human reactions shifted – those between masters and servants, husbands and wives, parents and children. And when human relations change, there is at the same time a change in religion, conduct, politics and literature.[2]

The date is a matter for argument (1910 is too late and the 1900s were the radical decade, in my view), but Virginia Woolf was right about the facts.

Brandes's book is remembered for another reason. The essay which it contained on Henrik Ibsen (1828–1906) was the first to make the Norwegian playwright known to a wider audience. There could be no more appropriate figure with whom to introduce my account of the 'modern period', which overlaps with the late Victorian age and runs on into the 1930s.

Recognized by everyone today as the founder of modern drama, at the time between the 1880s and his death in 1906 Ibsen was the centre of a storm of controversy. What offended the critics and galvanized the young was his boldness in making the theatre a place for the serious discussion of moral and social issues, not wrapped up in historical disguise but taken from contemporary life and presented directly, without comment or explanation, through a mastery of dialogue which has never been surpassed. Ibsen was a moralist who reacted angrily against the shams and illusions with which men and women deceived themselves and each other. Like Euripides he questioned the moral and

91–99 Ibsen, Freud, Jung, Stravinsky, Thomas Mann, Max Weber, Einstein, Picasso, Bertrand Russell

social beliefs of his time, exposing the gap between the rhetoric and the reality, confronting his audiences with situations in which they recognized – or angrily resisted recognizing – themselves.

But Ibsen was an artist and refused to become a prophet. He resisted every attempt to identify him with causes, parties and reforms – including Ibsenism. He had no faith in such activities. 'My calling', he declared, 'is to question, not to answer.'

Ibsen's art lies in observing and penetrating human character and human relationships in a search for authenticity. No writer ever created a more memorable series of feminine characters, but when the Norwegian Society for Women's Rights gave a banquet for him, he replied to their toast by saying:

I have been more of a poet and less of a social philosopher than people tend to suppose. I must disclaim the honour of having consciously worked for women's rights. I am not even quite sure what women's rights really are. To me it has been a question of human rights . . . Of course it is incidentally desirable to solve the problem of women; but that has not been my object. My task has been the portrayal of human beings.[3]

It is Ibsen's insistence on his independence as an artist that has given his plays their power to speak to us still a hundred years later, but what many wanted at the time was a prophet with a message.

Some believed they had found him in Friedrich Nietzsche (1844–1900). Virtually unknown until 1888, when he too was brought to the attention of a European audience in a lecture by Georg Brandes, he created a sensation by the force with which he did not question but rejected the whole of nineteenth-century civilization and its values. Although he had a poor opinion of human beings in the mass, Ibsen belongs to the humanist tradition because he believed in the individual human personality and its power to learn from suffering and rise above circumstances, and because of his passion for freedom – not the possession but the pursuit of freedom. Nietzsche, on the other hand, despised humanism, both in its classical Goethean form of balance and restraint, and in its utilitarian-rationalist version.

In his earlier book *The Birth of Tragedy* (1872) he had shown his originality by demonstrating the extent to which Greek culture had embraced the dark, irrational Dionysian elements in human life as well as the rational Apollonian face on which so much emphasis had been laid. Ten years later (in *The Gay Science*), in words which he assigned to the character of the Madman he himself was to assume, Nietzsche declared: 'God is dead! God remains dead! and we have killed Him! How shall we comfort ourselves – we who are the greatest murderers of all?'[4] He went on to denounce the 'slave morality' of Christianity as well as reason and the values of the Enlightenment. In their place he preached the master morality of the Will to Power.

Nietzsche's extraordinary impact was due to his ability to put into words the impulse many intellectuals and writers in the late nineteenth century felt to break with an over-organized and over-rationalized civilization, and to exalt instinct and emotion over reason. The fact that he himself was shortly afterwards stricken with the insanity which crippled him for the rest of his life (1889–1900) did not detract from the power of his vision that mankind had reached a breaking point in which all values would be re-cast.

The fascination with the irrational to which Nietzsche appealed in the 1890s and 1900s found expression in a variety of different forms: in Bergson's intuitionism; Sorel's myth of violence; the response to Freud's exploration of the unconscious and dreams; the aesthetic cult of 'Art for Art's sake', beginning with Baudelaire, and continued by Verlaine, Stefan George and Rilke; the plunge into an experimentalism which accepted no limits and was characterized by Rimbaud as 'a disordering of the senses'.

Such a change of direction posed a direct threat to the humanist tradition which, when it had pressed the claims of the imagination against an over-reliance on reason, had seen – as Goethe, the one-time author of *The Sorrows of Werther*, urged – the need to balance and check the subjective with the objective faculties of the mind.

If I choose Strindberg, born in 1849, to represent this change it is because, although he died in 1912, he appears, to an unusual degree, to be orientated towards and to prefigure the sensibility of the post-war world. He had enthusiastically welcomed Nietzsche's iconoclasm, and when Nietzsche wrote to him, in December 1888, that he now felt

possessed of the strength 'to cleave the history of mankind in two', Strindberg had no doubt on which side of the divide he would be. He was moved by an urge to fragmentation, to the breaking up of events, of consciousness and of characters. In the preface to his play *Miss Julie*, published the same year, 1888, he wrote of the figures he had created,

Since they are modern characters, living in an age of transition more urgently hysterical at any rate than the age which preceded it, I have drawn them as split and vacillating. They are conglomerations of past and present, bits from books and newspapers, scraps of humanity, rags and tatters of fine clothing, patched together as in the human soul.[5]

Strindberg's wide-ranging mind left few areas of human consciousness or activity unexplored: his complete works in Swedish run to 55 volumes and his temperament is described as 'by stages radical, iconoclast, sceptic, mystic, devout'. His life followed an erratic course, including three unsuccessful marriages and his own personal 'Inferno' crisis, a nervous breakdown which he claimed made him familiar with the dimensions of Hell, and which he turned to good account in his later plays such as *The Ghost Sonata* (1907).

Strindberg became increasingly scornful of Ibsen and his success. The older man recognized that the Swede possessed 'a very great talent' and told an interviewer that when he read *Inferno*, it had 'made a very powerful impression on me'. But Ibsen, although he understood as well as any man who ever wrote the irrational forces at work in human beings (he was not Freud's favorite author for nothing), did not believe, any more than Freud, in giving them free rein in his own life. He distrusted Strindberg's instability of behaviour and opinions and bought a portrait of him by Christian Krohg (which he called 'Insanity Emerging' – see p. 136) and hung it in his study. It helped him to work, he said, 'to have that madman staring down at me. . . . He is my mortal enemy, and shall hang there and watch while I write.'[6]

It was after 1914 that Strindberg came into his own, when he found a more receptive audience created by the disorientation and break-up of traditional values that followed the War. He then emerged as 'a private, intimate, prophetic embodiment of a *malaise* that is wholly and recognisably modern'.[7] His importance for my theme is that, by the same token, he can be taken as the harbinger of a twentieth-century crisis of humanism as severe as that of the sixteenth century and the Wars of Religion, when a world lost to reason and humanity spurned the humanism of the Renaissance.

2

You will notice that I use the phrase 'modern period' rather than 'modern movement'. I do so because every attempt to characterize it or confine it within a formula has proved unsuccessful. The one thing you can say about the extraordinarily diverse art, thought and literature of the period is that they are 'modern', no more. But as an identification this means a lot, for it points to the widely shared contemporary feeling that those who were alive then were living in wholly novel times; that their experience was unique; that continuity with the past had been broken and that they had to work out new values and forms of expression for themselves. In short, the essence of modernism was a new consciousness, new ways of seeing man and the world, a condition of the human mind for which there was no precedent. Whether this is how it appears now is another question; there is no doubt that it was a view held with passionate conviction by many of the most creative people of the time and that it inspired a remarkable burst of innovation in science, literature, the arts, the human and social sciences.

The difficulty in even describing the period, let alone attempting to characterize it, is to get the balance between the different elements right. Summing up their own attempt, Malcolm Bradbury and James McFarlane write:

In short, Modernism was in most countries an extraordinary compound of the futuristic and the nihilistic, the revolutionary and the conservative, the naturalistic and the symbolistic, the romantic and the classical. It was a celebration of a technological age and a condemnation of it; an excited acceptance of the belief that the old regimes of culture were over, and a deep despairing in the face of that fear. . . .[8]

They add: 'This crucial compound [elsewhere described as 'Janus-faced'] persists until after the War, and certainly up to 1930.'

At the beginning of this chapter I emphasized those elements in the mixture which express alienation and discontinuity, the replacement of reason, order, optimism by a vision of the world in terms of un-reason, fragmentation and frequently despair.

These are an essential part of the 'modern' consciousness as it developed between the 1880s and the 1930s and they are deeply impressed on us for two reasons. The first is 'the shock of the modern', that disturbing passion for innovation which led many people – and still leads some – to reject modern thought, modern art and architecture, modern literature and music *en bloc*, without discrimination, as marking the breakdown of Western civilization in anarchy. The second is that the view of the modern period as the onset of nihilism appears to be confirmed, beyond doubt, by European experience in the age that immediately follows, the age of Hitler (1889–1945) and Stalin (1879–1953).

Nonetheless, I believe that to see the modern period solely, or even predominantly, in these terms is misleading, again for two reasons. The first is that it telescopes history and ignores the fact that, as late as the mid-1930s, a majority of people living in the Western world either did not share, or resisted, the sense of crisis and despair felt by those who foresaw what was coming. The second is that the sense of vertigo, of the ground crumbling beneath one's feet, for which one can certainly find evidence throughout the period, was balanced by the excitement which others felt at the new horizons which were opening up. Not a few of the certainties called in question were in any case hollow and belonged to Matthew Arnold's 'one world already dead'. And Arnold's other world was no longer 'powerless to be born': it *was* a new world which was being born.

If there is one development to which the term 'new horizons' can be applied, it is to the revolution in physics which, following the discovery of X-rays by Röntgen and of radium by the Curies, began with Max Planck's formulation of the quantum theory in 1900. By 1915 it had already produced Rutherford's and Niels Bohr's new models of atomic structure and Einstein's special and general theories of relativity.

Apart from the extraordinary interest of the discoveries and ideas themselves, continued with Bohr's development of the 'complementarity' concept and Heisenberg's enunciation, in 1927, of 'the principle of indeterminacy', there are few episodes in history which can rival this as a sustained demonstration of what can be accomplished by the human mind when reason and imagination are combined at their peak, something reaching far beyond the positivists' stereotype of the scientific method.

What, however, were the implications of a scientific revolution comparable in scope with that which had culminated in Newton? Scientists were justifiably irritated at hearing Einstein's (1879–1955) principle of relativity devalued into a synonym for relativism and the denial of all objective truth, or Heisenberg's (1901–76) principle of indeterminacy vulgarized to vindicate free will against determinism. None the less the layman's instinct was not wrong in asking whether a fundamental change, of more than technical importance, had not taken place. The work of the previous generation of Kelvin (1824–1907) and Clerk-Maxwell (1831–79) had appeared to bring within reach a comprehensive, unified picture of the physical universe. If that was now called in question, what happened to the positivist, materialist view of the universe which rested its claims on what was believed to be the most secure achievement of scientific thought?

As Western civilization benefited more and more from the application of science to its problems through technology, it made little difference in practice: the prestige of science and Western societies' dependence on it were not affected.

But for the more philosophically-minded, including those who were scientists, the question that remained unanswered was whether the unified picture of the universe presented by classical physics would at some stage be replaced by a new unified model, as Einstein himself believed, but failed to achieve. Or whether Ernst Mach (1838–1916), the Austrian philosopher of science, might prove to have been right when, as early as the 1880s, he had argued that science was a practical activity and that the function of scientific laws and concepts was not to represent reality, but to provide a necessary, but hypothetical, framework which the scientist required for his work. They were not to be erected into absolutes, the mistake metaphysics made, but treated as neither true nor false but useful. The fact that such questions could be asked opened up the possibility of a dialogue between science and other forms of the human search for the understanding of experience, such as the arts and the humanities, which had been ruled out by the dogmatic positivism of Mach's own day.

I shall try to show later why I believe that such a dialogue is still crucial for the development of a twentieth-century version of humanism. But let me first go on to look at other new departures of a different sort, beginning with politics and the study of society.

3

In this same period of 1890–1914, a new generation of liberals and social democrats combined to break finally with the prohibition which nineteenth-century liberalism, in the name of *laissez-faire*, had placed on intervention by the state in the social problems created by industrialization and the growth of cities. By 1914 the earlier initiatives of Bismarck's Reich in establishing national insurance had been taken up and extended in other Western countries, including Britain and France. The social legislation introduced by the British liberal governments of 1906–16, for example, with its provision for insurance against sickness, workmen's compensation against accidents and old age pensions, reflected – although it was far from satisfying – the new radicalism preached, with individual variations, by Graham Wallas, the Hammonds, L. T. Hobhouse, J. A. Hobson and the Fabians.[9] This in turn pointed forward to the moral arguments in favour of socialism presented by R. H. Tawney in *The Acquisitive Society* (1921) – a book which had a greater impact than Marx on the British Labour Party's thinking – to the Keynesian revolution in economic policy of the 1930s, and the welfare state, for which Beveridge's wartime Report of 1942 provided the intellectual justification.

The new agenda of twentieth-century politics which this inaugurated, giving priority to social and economic issues, owed much to the development of sociology. The systematic study of society of which Montesquieu and Adam Smith had laid the foundations, and to which Karl Marx had added new dimensions of his own, aroused a host of prejudices by the sort of questions it asked and the propositions it put forward. The reasons for this critical reception of sociology (as for its later uncritical acceptance) form a fascinating chapter in intellectual and social history. The prejudices, however, should not obscure the strong claim any study has to be considered as part of the humanist tradition which sets as its object to investigate and understand how human beings adapt to the novel and constantly changing conditions of modern industrialized societies. It may be a claim which by no means all sociologists would wish to make, and which some would repudiate. As an historian, however, while recognizing the differences in method and aims between them, I have no doubt that the separation of the social sciences and the humanities from each other, and particularly of sociology and history, has only impoverished both.

In justification of my view that sociology and anthropology on the one hand, and history on the other, are naturally complementary to each other, let me mention some of the insights and the concepts developed by sociologists in the same creative period I am talking about (in the early years of the century) which have become part of the common stock of twentieth-century ideas. Among them are the non-rational elements (accident, prejudice and custom) which Graham Wallas (1858–1932) identified in *Human Nature in Politics* (1908); and the distinction which the Italians Pareto (1848–1923) and Mosca (1858–1941) found in all societies between a ruling class or élite, however its power is justified or disguised, and the masses who are ruled – with the complementary concept of the circulation of élites which led Pareto to characterize history as 'the graveyard of aristocracies'. The contrast which the German sociologist Ferdinand Tönnies (1855–1936) drew between *Gemeinschaft* (a natural community, governed by folkways, mores and religion) and *Gesellschaft* (a society governed by rational arrangements embodied in laws and contracts) has become as much a part of intellectual currency as 'élite', and as the concept of 'conspicuous consumption' which the American Thorstein Veblen (1857–1929) created in his *Theory of the Leisure Class* (1899).

The two leading figures in the formative period of modern sociology took very different views of its methods and objectives. Emile Durkheim (1858–1917), in the tradition of French rationalism, showed a distrust of history and a preference for proceeding by definition and analysis; Max Weber (1864–1920), in the tradition of German historicism, showed a distrust of definitions and preferred to ground his theoretical propositions in specific historical situations.

Both men were attracted by the study of religion. Durkheim was less interested in the content of religion, belief in the supernatural or personal experience, than in its social function, which, he believed, had its beginning in totemism. He saw society as a moral order at the core of which was a set of values, a 'collective consciousness', of which religion was the symbolic representation, with the function of maintaining the line drawn between the sacred and the profane.

Moving away from an historical view of how society developed, Durkheim postulated two types of social solidarity. The first was 'mechanical' (a very different use of the term from that which we encountered in the earlier nineteenth century), a traditional society in which there was little division of labour and men accepted common norms. In the second, 'organic' (again a very different use), functions became specialized; instead of the family, the workplace became the focus of attachment, and the *conscience collective* was threatened with disintegration, producing the state of *anomie*, or disorientation, which Durkheim saw as the characteristic *malaise* of modern society, expressing itself in such symptoms as industrial class conflict. If religion could no longer fulfil its traditional role of sustaining a common moral code, a substitute would have to be created, and Durkheim looked to moral education and citizenship to produce this in the form of a set of values relating to man's common humanity. The importance of this is underlined by the fact that Durkheim rejected the individualist assumptions of English social thought, arguing that society is prior to the individual and that the social cannot be reduced to the psychological, a thesis which he illustrated by his study of suicide (1897).

Weber's very different interest took him to a comparative study of the historic religions, such as those of India and China, ancient Judaism and Protestantism, seeking light on the specific question why capitalism should have developed in the West rather than elsewhere, e.g. in Asia. His answer was 'the Protestant ethic', on which he wrote his most famous book,[10] arguing that religious might rival economic factors as dynamic influences on social development. This was a specific example of his general thesis that human behaviour was too rich and complex to be capable of explanation by any single factor, such as Marx and Engels had claimed for their materialist interpretation of history; it required a more pluralistic view of the *interpenetration* of ideas, whether religious or secular, with economic and social interests.

Weber saw increasing rationalization as the destructive characteristic of modern society, a process common to both capitalism and socialism, which he identified with 'the iron law of bureaucracy' and (borrowing the word from Schiller) with *Entzauberung*, the expulsion of magic from the universe and human life.

As opposed to Durkheim's positivist approach, Weber insisted that the meanings individuals attach to their activities are essential to understanding them. But he went beyond the historicism of Dilthey and Rickert, in which he had been brought up, to argue that it was also possible to establish causal-functional, or general explanations, by the use of the comparative method and the concept of 'ideal types'. An example of the latter is the distinction he made between ideal types of traditional, rational-legal and charismatic authority. This desire to bring together opposing views (which recalls the later Mill) is reflected in Weber's argument that there was nothing inconsistent in combining scientific objectivity in the study of society and in clarification of the choices which had to be made, with a recognition that men's decisions between these would express their subjective value preferences.

In effect, Durkheim and Weber represent the same two rival claims to represent the humanist tradition which I identified in my lecture on the nineteenth century, one positivist-rationalist-scientific in its outlook, bent upon preserving its autonomy from what was seen as the subjective confusion of history and the humanities, the other seeking to combine them.

4

Not only human society but individual human nature was being looked at in new ways. Nineteenth-century psychology, after Darwin, had been closely identified with physiology and the experimental

investigation of the physical bases of mental processes. That great popularizer, T. H. Huxley, summed up the assumptions on which it was based when he said in 1872: 'We are conscious automata', and went on to describe this as a wonderfully simplifying explanation. 'The consciousness of brutes would appear to be related to the mechanism of their body simply as a collateral product of its workings . . . and the argumentation which applies to brutes holds good of men.'[11]

Whatever else the newcomers – William James, Freud, Jung, Adler – might disagree about, they were agreed in rejecting such a view and insisting that consciousness could not be reduced to, or 'explained', in terms of the physical operations of the brain and the nervous system.

In 1890, after qualifying as a doctor and spending nearly twenty years in research and teaching in experimental psychology at Harvard, William James (1842–1910, the elder brother of Henry James) published *The Principles of Psychology*, a book which still ranks as a classic. His object was to investigate and describe thoughts and feelings *as experienced*. Of course, these occur in a physical environment existing in space and time with which they coexist and which in some sense they 'know'. But James declined to speculate in what sense, showing in a

102 The brothers Henry (left) and William James, photographed in 1905

brilliant survey of theories of mind since Plato how the import from philosophy of explanations of their relationship with the physical world – whether materialist, idealist, associationist or evolutionist – clouded psychological observation and distorted it to fit a preconceived pattern. Freed from such metaphysical preoccupations and starting from 'consciousness-as-we-feel-it', James proceeded to show how much could be learned about neglected aspects of intelligence, feelings, habit and memory, how rich and subtle was the flow of what he named 'the stream of consciousness' – a process, not a substance, a function not to be 'explained' in terms other than its own. By his combination of observation and argument, James successfully challenged the associationist view of psychology which had dominated British empiricism since Locke, and the dualism of 'knower' and 'known', of the mind copying external objects, which had been a postulate of psychology and philosophy since Descartes.

William James seems to me to have been underestimated, partly because of a wit and racy style which his friend C. S. Peirce, from whom he borrowed the term 'Pragmatism', deplored as inappropriate to the discussion of serious philosophical questions; partly because that term (which he first used for a volume of lectures written only four years before his death) has been used to label him ever since as the practical man's philosopher and parodied by making his test of truth the impatient American's question, Does it work?[12]

One work of James's which has never lost its interest is *The Varieties of Religious Experience*, the Gifford Lectures delivered in Edinburgh in 1901–02. Not only do these demonstrate the psychological insight he could bring to exploring a subject which Freud was to dismiss out of hand as a harmful illusion, but they are a striking example of what he meant by the pragmatic approach in seeking the meaning and value of any idea – scientific and philosophical as well as religious – in the consequences to which it leads. Bertrand Russell's acid remark that, if James were right, 'theories become instruments not answers to enigmas' missed the point. This was just what James believed – and a very defensible view it is, as A. N. Whitehead saw, of the function of a scientific theory in the new physics.

Refusing to accept the notion, which he denounced as a philosophical idol, of a ready-made 'reality', complete from eternity and independent of human thinking, James saw the universe as a process forever in the making, the meaning and values of which men themselves create.

There is no danger of anyone underrating Freud (1856–1939), whose work, beginning with *The Interpretation of Dreams* in 1900, gives him a fair claim to be regarded as the most original, certainly the most influential thinker of the first half of the twentieth century. Both in his originality and in his influence there is an obvious parallel with Darwin. Both men took a concept which was in the air at the time, in one case evolution, in the other the unconscious, and transformed it into the centrepiece of a revolutionary new view, of biology in Darwin's case, of psychology in Freud's. Their extraordinary influence is to be accounted for in the same way. After powerful initial resistance to Darwin's theories, a widespread conviction formed in the popular mind that he had *proved*, not only that men were descended from apes, but that the universal law of evolution was a struggle for survival in which the fittest came out on top and the weak were eliminated. In Freud's case – again after powerful initial resistance – a similar conviction formed that he had proved scientifically that unhappiness was neurotic and that neurosis was caused by sexual repression; ergo, if men and women were to be happy, their sexual instincts must be given free play.

The fact that Freud's unique impact on the thought and culture of our time has in large part been due to a vulgarized version of his ideas does not detract from his achievement. The popular view was not wrong in believing that his 'discovery' of the unconscious has revolutionized our view of human nature, an achievement all the greater because of the opposition and vilification Freud had to overcome in challenging the most deep-rooted of all taboos, that against the open discussion of sex.

But has he a place in the humanist tradition? If he refused to accept physical explanations of states of mind, he can certainly be described as a determinist whose model of the unconscious and its relations with the conscious mind is mechanistic and based on a belief in the primacy of the sexual instincts (he later added a further primal instinct of aggression) which he defended with dogmatic tenacity. Freud had a poor opinion of human beings, whom he considered essentially irrational creatures, using reason to deceive themselves about their true nature by ingenious rationalization or by cloaking themselves in such illusions as religious belief.

On the other hand, it can be argued that Freud, instead of vindicating irrationality or exalting it as Nietzsche did, was not content to make the point that the unconscious did not follow the usual rules of logic but attempted, by the use of his own rational powers, to define the strange rules by which its own special kind of logic operated. Freud's own personal and family life was happy; and far from welcoming, he describes himself as struggling against and having to steel himself to accept the conclusions – for example, about infantile sexuality and the Oedipus complex – which he reached in his analysis of himself and his patients. He saw himself as the lonely explorer of a submerged and alarming world, finding courage to continue only in the humanist conviction that it was increased knowledge alone – particularly self-knowledge ('Know thyself') – that could set men free. If he adhered to a positivist-rationalist faith in facts, holding at arm's length all philosophical preconceptions and explanations, it was because he believed, as William James did, that it was only by sticking to 'the unconscious as experienced' (to paraphrase James) that he could keep the firm ground of 'reality' under his feet and not be lost in the mists of 'illusions', such as religion and art. He was convinced that it was only when men shed such illusions and recognized its unavoidable limitations that the frail but indispensable instrument of reason could operate.

In a letter which he wrote to the American neurologist, James J. Putnam, in the summer of 1915, Freud described himself as a highly moral man who accepted the ethical rules of modern civilization without question – all except those governing modern sexual conduct. 'Sexual morality, as society in its most extreme form defines it, seems to be very contemptible. I stand for an incomparably freer sexual life, although I myself have made very little use of such freedom: only in so far as I judged it to be allowable.'[13] Freud was not, as Heinz Hartmann says, 'a transvaluer of values – not in the sense, that is, that he wanted to impress on his fellow men a new scale of moral values.'[14] Freud was a moralist who sought to make men's values more effective by relieving them of the burden of sexual guilt and hypocrisy and the neuroses to which they lead. 'Experience', he wrote 'teaches that there is for most people a limit beyond which their constitution cannot comply with the demands of culture. All those who want to be nobler than their constitution permits lapse into neurosis.'[15]

It may well seem to some that the sexual revolution to which Freud contributed has gone too far towards permissiveness; but for anyone who has penetrated the dark, oppressive and unhappy world of Victorian sexuality, it seems to me that there can be little doubt that, with all its excesses, the change has been a liberation, especially for women. Freud himself was not optimistic about the future of mankind, especially after the First World War had led him to develop his concept of the death instinct (*Thanatos*, engaged in a life and death struggle with *Eros*). He could understand all too well, he wrote in *Civilisation and Its Discontents* (1930), the critic who suggested that 'the whole effort [of civilization] is not worth the trouble'. But he could see no alternative to the sacrifices civilization imposes on man's instinctual life or the restraints it applies to his aggressive instincts, if mankind was to survive. Peter Gay sums it up well when he writes:

Freud had no use whatever for the celebration of irrational forces, or for the primitivism that would evade the dialectic of civilisation by abandoning civilisation altogether. . . . He had not descended to the sewer of human nature to wallow in what he had found there. He was no devotee of the Id; he assigned no privileged position to that blind, imperious agent of the will, and valued the organising rationalism of the Ego, or the nay-saying constraints of the super-ego as equally natural.[16]

Freud, as I have said, found it necessary to believe that he was a scientist dealing only with facts, but it is scientists who have shown most reserve about his theories. Their view was summed up by an Oxford psychologist, B. A. Farrell, who acknowledged that Freud's work 'has revolutionised the popular view of human nature in the West (rather as Marx has changed our view of society)', but added that 'Freud's theoretical contribution has not yet been incorporated into science' and that it remains an open question 'whether he really turns out to be a Darwin of the human mind or only someone who, like a Ptolemy or a Mesmer, has led us up an interesting and important dead end.'[17] By contrast, his ideas, even at their most speculative, have from the beginning attracted the interest of writers and artists. This is no accident. Lionel Trilling (1905–75), in an essay on 'Freud and Literature' published in 1940,[18] pointed out that 'psychoanalysis is one of the culminations of the Romantic literature of the nineteenth century', and recalled Freud's response at the celebration of his seventieth birthday when he was acclaimed as 'the discoverer of the unconscious'. Freud disclaimed the title: 'The poets and philosophers before me discovered the unconscious. What I discovered was the scientific method by which the unconscious can be studied.'

Trilling goes on to argue that if one looks at the 'illogical logic' which Freud believed was the way in which the unconscious works – for example, its association of apparently incompatible ideas and images, and its preference for the concrete over the general, for the tangible trifle over the large abstraction, for the ambiguous over the precise – this describes something immediately recognizable by the poet and the artist as the way in which many poems and paintings, especially non-representational art, begin. Of all mental systems, he concludes, Freud's is the one 'which makes poetry indigenous to the very constitution of the mind', and, far from acting as a check on the creative faculties by narrowing and simplifying the human world for the artist, opens and complicates it. In short, whatever may be Freud's final place in the history of science, his place in the humanist tradition is assured by the affinity of his ideas with literature and the arts and his influence on them.

I am fortified in my belief that this is a valid view of Freud's work – whatever Freud himself would have thought of it – by its subsequent history. For it became clear as early as the breach between Freud and Adler (in 1911) and the famous quarrel between Freud and Jung (in 1913) that it is perfectly possible to separate Freud's great achievement in demonstrating he importance of the unconscious and identifying the royal road (as Jung called it) to its exploration through dreams, from the need to interpret all dreams or fantasies in terms of the patient's infantile sexuality or to suppose that the creative energy of the mind, the libido, is wholly sexual.

Alfred Adler (1870–1937) found the key in aggression to compensate for feelings of inferiority and regarded sex as an opportunity to express dominance. Carl Gustav Jung (1875–1961) went a different way. While agreeing that hysterical neuroses were generally connected with a sexual disturbance, Jung's experience with the more serious disorders of schizophrenia led him to believe that these disorders arise from a more general, not specifically sexual, failure in adaptation to external reality. As a result of his involvement with schizophrenics, he began to explore the idea of a substratum of mind common to all men, a collective unconscious underlying the personal, and responsible for the spontaneous production of myths, visions, certain kinds of dreams and religious ideas which Jung showed were to be found in a number of different cultures and periods of history.

One example of such primordial images or archetypes is the Hero who appears, with different features, in every mythology.[19] Jung's investigation of the functions of mythology led him to point out that in every age except our own, men and women have found meaning for their lives in some form of religion or myth, and to argue that many people today are suffering from a sense of futility because, although they have discarded traditional beliefs, they need, and can no longer find, a religion or myth to live by: hence the attraction of Communism, Nazism or Fascism as substitutes, and the proliferation of such cults as the Rastafarians.

While Freud concentrated on looking for the origin of psychological symptoms further back in some earlier experience, Jung came to see in much psychological material presented by disturbed patients a forward-looking attempt at compensation on the part of the unconscious for a one-sided, unbalanced attitude on the part of the conscious mind. From this, Jung developed the view that the inner world and its images, which Freudians saw as derived from infantile experience and as a hindrance to accepting reality, could actually be the source on which men and women draw for the means of adapting to the external world, whether this takes the form of religion, culture, art or science.

Jung became particularly interested in the problems of those who found themselves, often after success in their earlier years, depressed in mid-term by a sense of futility and lack of meaning in their lives. He believed that only by recognizing and accepting some higher authority or purpose than the Ego, by finding his or her own 'myth', could men and women overcome the conflicts in themselves and achieve what he called 'individuation', realizing their own unique selfhood.

Above the door of his house Jung carved a saying of the Delphic Oracle which read: VOCATUS ATQUE NON VOCATUS, DEUS ADERIT 'Invoked or not invoked, the god will be present'. The psychological function of religion, whatever its content, seemed as important to Jung as its social function had to Durkheim, and he devoted much of his time tg collecting diverse and arcane material, ranging from the Gnostics and the alchemists to the Chinese classic of meditation, *The Secret of the Golden Flower*, all of which are concerned with different versions of the same spiritual quest, the search for something greater than oneself, which he saw as the dominant feature and need of human beings once they had reached maturity.

Jung has never attracted the popular interest that Freud has done, and the dense, obscure style in which he writes, by comparison with Freud's clarity, does not make it easier to understand him. His critics accuse him of mysticism, vagueness and pseudo-science; his defenders claim that he offers a more open-minded interpretation of the unconscious, free from Freud's dogmatism and with the valuable addition of his exploration of a collective unconscious. I believe both have a place in the humanist tradition and it seems to me largely a matter of temperament and experience which one is attracted to. The point I want to underline is that recognition of the importance of the unconscious, the credit for which is Freud's, is compatible with more than one view of which element in it to lay most emphasis on – a conclusion that is hardly surprising in talking of an inner world of which the most obvious characteristic is its ambiguity.

5

While Freud and Jung were exploring the unconscious, a new generation of artists – beginning with *Les Fauves* and the Cubists in Paris, *Die Brücke* and *Der Blaue Reiter* groups in Germany – was responsible for the most spectacular outburst of innovation in the visual arts since the Renaissance. There was the same extraordinary concentration of experimentation and talent in those years as there had been in the Italian Renaissance. Among painters, to mention only the greatest, the later Cézanne (who died in 1906), Picasso, Braque, Matisse, Kandinsky, Mondrian, Klee, Munch, Léger. Among architects, Adolf Loos, Frank Lloyd Wright, Le Corbusier, Gropius, Mies van der Rohe, and the Bauhaus with its unique influence on modern design.

The freshness and impact of this early period could never be repeated, but the modern movement continued to expand and develop new ideas down to the Second World War. It was still capable of putting forth new branches even after the War, as witness the later flowering of modern art in England (Henry Moore, Barbara Hepworth, Ben Nicholson and Graham Sutherland). Perhaps even more impressive was the ability of the earlier generation of artists in old age to go on producing startling new work after the Second World War – Matisse's cut-out gouaches, produced when he was in his eighties and confined to bed, as well as the chapel at Vence; Corbusier's pilgrimage chapel at Ronchamp, and Chandigarh, the new capital of the Punjab; or, in music, Stravinsky's late move into serialism after his Neoclassical period, itself an abrupt change from the great innovatory scores – *The Firebird* and *The Rite of Spring* – which he had written for Diaghilev's Ballets Russes before 1914.

103 Taliesin West, which Frank Lloyd Wright built as a winter home for himself and his students in Arizona. Named after a Welsh bard of the 6th century, it was begun in 1938 and continually renovated and added to until his death in 1959 (see note on p. 202)

The one characteristic these highly individualistic artists and architects and musicians would ever have accepted as something they had in common was the desire to break out from the conventions of the nineteenth century. These, even when they had been the product of earlier rebellions, had now become restrictive, laying down with a dead hand what could be accepted as art (when Picasso (1881–1973) was asked 'What is art?', he replied 'What isn't?') or what could be regarded as architecture or music.

The Spanish humanist, Ortega y Gasset (1883–1955), saw in the innovations of the modern movement 'the dehumanization of art'. It is a view I do not share. If I spend a morning at the Guggenheim Museum and in the marvellous space created by Frank Lloyd Wright walk slowly down past the line of Kandinsky's canvases; if I recall walking, stunned, out of the Picasso Retrospective, or standing in the garden at St Ives which Barbara Hepworth created to provide a setting for her sculpture, I have the same lift and exhilaration of spirit that I feel when I go back to Florence or Rome and see the art that expressed the humanism of the Renaissance. The fact that the art of the moderns is often non-representational I see as an extension, not a contraction, of art. Paul Klee's fantasies delight me. In the severe lines of an abstract painting by Mondrian or Ben Nicholson I find the same deep satisfaction as in every other work of art (in music and ballet as well as painting and sculpture) when it reveals the hidden order underlying the permanent flux – in this case expressed in its simplest terms.

What distinguishes the work of the great modern architects from the anonymous slab-like tower blocks which deface our cities is precisely the attention masters like Frank Lloyd Wright,[20] Mies van der Rohe and Alvar Aalto paid to human scale and the environment in which people live and work. In taking over the directorship of the Bauhaus, Walter Gropius (1883–1969) declared his ambition to reconcile art and technology, 'to eliminate every drawback of the machine without sacrificing any of its real advantages.' After the lush eclecticism of nineteenth-century architecture, the proportions and spare lines of a well-designed modern building express for me a reversion to the classical principles of architecture in a contemporary form.[21]

Now that we can begin to see their achievements in perspective, it is clear that the moderns' break with the past in painting and sculpture was less complete than it seemed at the time – exactly the same conclusion that scholars have reached about the Renaissance, re-establishing the continuities that linked the artists and writers of the fourteenth and fifteenth centuries to the Middle Ages from which they felt themselves to be breaking free. While unquestionably revolutionary – as Renaissance art had also been – the modern period, far from destroying or abandoning altogether the Western tradition in the arts, seems to me to have added a brilliant new chapter to it.

Many artists were aware of and explored their relationship with their predecessors. In 1957, for example, when he was in his mid-seventies, Picasso produced the astonishing series of some twenty variations on the theme of Velasquez' masterpiece *Las Meninas* (The Ladies-in-Waiting) which his Spanish predecessor had painted three hundred years before, · in 1656, and which Picasso had studied and thought about for twenty years. Stravinsky (1882–1971) in his Neoclassical period studied in depth and drew in the same entirely original way on the music of Handel (*Oedipus Rex*, 1927), Bach (the violin concerto of 1931) and Mozart (*The Rake's Progress*, 1951). Le Corbusier (1887–1965), in his famous book *Vers une architecture* (1923), the bible of modernist architecture in which he set out the principles of a 'machine aesthetic', went back to the ancient Greeks for a modular system of design based on the Golden Section, and followed Alberti and Leonardo da Vinci in making the proportions of the human body the basis of his own Modulor.

The twentieth century added two new visual arts, photography and the film, both of which enjoyed the great advantage from the beginning of being able to use the techniques of mass communication and thus

104 Le Corbusier's drawing to illustrate his Modulor

105 A scene from one of the most famous of early films, Fritz Lang's *Metropolis*, 1925–26, a protest against the dehumanization of man by industry

106 A very different kind of protest against the same threat: Charlie Chaplin's satire on factory life, *Modern Times*, made in 1936

naturally to reflect and adapt themselves to a mass society. When I was a student studying Greek and Roman civilization at Oxford in the 1930s, the classic films I saw seemed to me as natural a part of my introduction to the humanist tradition as reading Thucydides and Aristotle.[22] Like the film director, the photographer – a Stieglitz, a Cartier-Bresson – seizes upon the particularity of human lives and extends into the faceless mass society of our times the humanist tradition of individual portraiture. Nothing made this clearer for me than the famous exhibition which Edward Steichen organized for the Museum of Modern Art in 1955

152

under the title of 'The Family of Man' and which was subsequently shown throughout the world. My sons' generation would add a third to film and photography, the demotic art of jazz, which shares with them the same ability to pass effortlessly through the barriers of race, language and class, and speak to all men and women.

6

By no means all the artists in the generation I am speaking of had an affinity with humanism. This is particularly true if one brings literature into the reckoning. Great poet though he was, W. B. Yeats (1865–1939), for example, looked to a quite different, mystical-archaic-heroic, tradition which distrusted reason and felt the same aversion to a modern world born out of the Enlightenment as T. S. Eliot, Ezra Pound and Paul Claudel. Alienation from a hated bourgeois society, attraction to the irrational as a deeper and more penetrating approach to experience, the influence of Nietzsche – all the themes of the late nineteenth-century revolt, often combined with bold experiments in style, were still to be heard in the literature of the twentieth century.

On the one hand, it produced such masterpieces of despair as Kafka's *The Castle* and *The Trial*.[23] With 'a disposition akin to madness, separated from it only by a writing table' (Erich Heller),[24] Kafka (1883–1924) experienced in advance, in his imagination, and expressed with unequalled subtlety, the nightmare reality which was to descend like an evil cloud on Central Europe. Or the plays of Pirandello (1867–1936), collected under the title of *Naked Masks* – man is only able truly to be himself when wearing the mask which lets him feel free to discard pretence. In these plays every variation on the theme of the discontinuity of identity ('I am what people think I am,' the wife says in *Right You Are, If You Think You Are*), the indeterminacy of truth, the wavering borderlines between truth and illusion, between sanity and madness, are played out with a pitiless logic.[25]

On the other hand, in D. H. Lawrence's (1885–1930) novels and poems the modern period produced an exaltation of the instinctual forces in man, expressed in a sexuality which was stifled by the repressions of civilization. Or later (as in surrealism), a scorn not only for reason but for humanity – in Sartre's *La Nausée* (1938), a disgust – which mocks the absurdity of men and women's efforts to raise themselves from the mud.

But this is to take too narrow and one-sided a view.

The literature and art of the modern period had to find forms in which to express a double revolution which they had helped to bring about. The first was the open recognition – or renewed recognition (it can hardly be called a discovery) – of the divided nature of man and of the role non-rational elements play in individual human lives and in the relationships that make up society. The second corresponding change was the recognition of the fragmentation of consciousness, the ambiguity of experience, the relativization of the truth. I suggest that you do not have to look far to find other writers (Thomas Mann and William Faulkner, to take two strongly contrasted examples), as gifted as any of those I have mentioned already, who take up these new and disturbing themes without either turning their backs on the modern world and giving way to despair, or abandoning (any more than Freud does) that fragile but indispensable thread of reason on which they depended to find their way out of the labyrinth.

As for the other theme, the stream of consciousness, and how it is to be represented in all the richness and complexity suggested by William James's description, there is no need to look further than Marcel Proust (1871–1922), with all the subtlety he brings to distinguishing between different kinds of time, asking, for example, why the memory of an occurrence provides a more concentrated impression of reality than the event itself. The obvious companion to *La Recherche du Temps Perdu* is that other masterpiece devoted to the recovery of the past, this time no more than twenty-four hours of Dublin life in the summer of 1904, James Joyce's *Ulysses*. Both Proust and Joyce (1882–1941) were searching for answers to the same question in relation to the internal world of consciousness as Picasso and Braque in relation to the external world: what happens when you change the conventions of representation, when you say as Picasso did, 'I paint forms as I think them, not as I see them'? No more, however, in the case of Proust and Joyce than in that of Picasso and Braque is the result a reduction, it is an expansion of consciousness, as of representation. The occurrences they recall are as commonplace as the objects the Cubists painted; but what they make of them is magic.

It is with writers and artists like these in mind that I believe Peter Gay is justified when he says of the modernist period that it found as many ways of affirming life as of rejecting it: 'Its bursting of boundaries did not imply hostility to discipline; its vigorous aesthetic and social criticism did not involve a yielding to depression: its profound exploration of unreason was not a celebration of irrationality.'[26]

I do not claim that the developments which we have glanced at between 1900 and 1940 – in science, politics, sociology, psychology, the arts and literature – constitute a phase of the humanist tradition comparable with those of the Renaissance and the Enlightenment. The time was too short for that. But the humanism which was threatened by the crisis of the mid-twentieth century was not the same as the liberal optimism and rationalism which had passed its zenith by the 1900s. It had broken away from that to adjust itself to a radical shift in consciousness and to new ways of looking at man and society, and at the same time had retained the link with reason, the discipline of thought and art which had been the hallmarks of the humanist tradition in the past. The elements of a new version of humanism had begun to come together. What happened to it is a question we shall have to leave until we have looked more closely at the nature of the crisis which overtook it at the end of the 1930s.

7

Before I turn to that, it would be an advantage to look back over the ground we have covered from the Renaissance, through the Enlightenment and the nineteenth century up to the Second World War, and try to bring together the main characteristics of the humanist tradition as my generation inherited it in the 1930s.

I repeat what I said at the beginning of my first lecture, that humanism is not a philosophical system or creed, but a continuing debate in which very different views have been and still are presented. There is nothing surprising in this. Divergent views are equally characteristic of Christianity, Buddhism, Islam – and Marxism. And of course there are limits to what can be counted, or claim to be, humanist. For example, I would not, myself, regard as humanist any view which is determinist or reductionist in its view of human life and consciousness, or which is authoritarian and intolerant. But within such limits debate is free and continues: it does not issue in final answers that settle the matter.

For the same reason no one has the right to say that his view of the humanist tradition is definitive; it can only be a personal one. But granted that, to me its most important and constant characteristics seem to be the following:

First, by contrast with a theological view of man (which sees him as part of a divine order) or the scientific (which sees him as part of a natural order), and in neither case central to it, humanism focuses on man, and starts from human experience. It argues indeed that this is all men and women have to go on, that this is the only answer to Montaigne's question, *Que sais-je?* That does not rule out either a religious belief in a divine order or the scientific investigation of man as part of a natural order but it makes the point that, like every other belief – including the values we live by, and indeed all our knowledge – they are derived by human minds from human experience.

The second characteristic humanist belief is that the individual human being has a value in him or herself – we still use the Renaissance phrase, the dignity of man – and that it is respect for this which is the source of all other values and of human rights. This respect is based upon the latent powers which men and women, and they alone, possess: the power to create and communicate (language, the arts, sciences, institutions), the power to observe themselves, to speculate, imagine, and reason.

Once liberated, these powers enable men and women to exercise a degree of freedom of choice and will, to change course, to innovate and thus to open the possibility – I underline possibility, not more than that, not certainty – of improving themselves and the human lot.

In order to liberate these powers and so enable men and women to develop their potential, two things are necessary. One is education, designed not as a training in specific tasks or techniques, but as an awakening to the possibilities of human life, a drawing out or cultivation of a young man's or young woman's human-ness. Some people are born with this awareness and their potentialities unfold naturally. But for the majority it needs to be evoked. Hence not only the central importance humanists have always attributed to education but also the broad terms in which they have conceived it as grounded in a general education, aimed at the all-round development of the personality and of the full range of an individual's talents.

The second condition on which the release of human energies depends is individual freedom. The eighteenth-century *philosophes* used the weapon of reason to get rid of the constraints and prohibitions imposed by custom, archaic laws and authoritarian institutions, both lay and ecclesiastical, and to dispel the fears and superstitions exploited by the Church and the whole apparatus of revealed religion. They sought to replace these by a reformed legal system, based on equality before the law, freedom of thought and freedom of opinion; and by a secular state, governed by representative institutions, with the injunction to legislate and interfere with individual freedom and individual enterprise as little as possible.

How little is a question on which the early nineteenth century and the twentieth have taken different views, and this illustrates the importance of looking at the humanist tradition historically, as a continuing debate. If one can appeal to the humanist and liberal tradition at one stage of its development in favour of *laissez-faire* policies, one can also appeal to the same tradition at a later stage for their rejection, and in justification of intervention to enlarge freedom by promoting social reforms, by curbing economic power and by providing for the basic human needs of those who cannot provide for themselves. Such differences of opinion on how far intervention by the state should go – and can go without becoming counterproductive – remain one of the characteristics of the humanist tradition. Far from being a weakness, this capacity to respond to changes in society and circumstances seems to me an advantage by comparison with the commitment to an inflexible orthodoxy.

A third characteristic of the tradition is the importance it has always attached to ideas, maintaining on the one hand that ideas are neither formed nor can be understood in isolation from their social or historical context; on the other that they cannot be reduced to the rationalization of individual economic or class interests, or of sexual and other instinctual drives. Max Weber's concept of the interpenetration of ideas, circumstances and interests comes closest to summing up the humanist view of ideas as neither wholly autonomous nor wholly derivative.

From the outburst of Petrarch against scholasticism in the fourteenth century, humanism has shown itself distrustful of the elaboration of abstract ideas in philosophical systems – whether theological, metaphysical or materialist. It has valued reason not for its system-building but for its critical and pragmatic application to the problems encountered in concrete human experience – moral, psychological, social and political. For the same reason it has shown a preference for historical over philosophical-analytical modes of explanation – or at least, as Max Weber argued, in combination with these – relating the universal human experiences to their expression in particular historical and cultural contexts. Instead of seeking to impose a single set of values or symbols – Catholic, Calvinist, Islamic, Marxist – it has accepted that there is more than one way to truth, and that those developed by other civilizations, whether in the past or the present – ancient Greek, Chinese, Roman, French, Indian – are to be taken seriously and an effort made to understand them in their own terms, even when we cannot accept them for ourselves, and may, because of their aggressive intolerance, be driven to defend our own values against them.

Humanism began in fourteenth- and fifteenth-century Italy with just such an attempt to penetrate and recover the remote world of Greek and Roman antiquity. Four centuries later Goethe repeated the experience and drew from it the inspiration to reshape his own life and art. The vitality of ancient Greek thought, literature and art is far from exhausted, as shown by the power the Oedipus myth still possessed for Freud and Stravinsky. We may regret that classical civilization is no longer familiar or accessible to many educated people. But what matters far more is that the effort of projecting oneself into the thoughts and feelings of other peoples – be they ancient Greeks, Chinese, Spanish or American Indians – or into earlier phases of our own society, through the study of their language, their history, their art and their beliefs, should not be allowed to disappear. This art of empathy – which Dilthey called *Verstehen* – is central to humanistic education and of the greatest value in breaking down the provinciality of knowing nothing about any other time or any other culture than one's own. Language and the power of communication through talk, through literature, drama, oratory and song are at the heart of the humanist tradition. So too is humour, from the Greek vase painters to Charlie Chaplin, one of the most distinctive forms of communication, the unique capacity men and women possess to laugh at themselves and other people, and to see the comical as well as the tragic side of the human predicament.

The arts have a special affinity with humanism, and this applies as much to music and dance and the other non-verbal arts – painting, sculpture, pottery – as to literature and drama, because of their power to pass through and communicate across the barriers of separate languages. In the seventeenth century Vico pointed out that symbols and myths express a society's beliefs and values, as one can see from the customs and conventions concerned with the universal experiences of birth, marriage and death, or again from a society's laws and institutions, such as property and the family. Here is another incredibly rich source to which the study of the humanities and of anthropology and sociology provide access, and on which the humanist tradition draws.

One of the oldest subjects of humanist discussion, already familiar in antiquity before being revived in Renaissance Italy is whether an active or a contemplative life is the better. In times of adversity, when living for example under a one-party regime provides little opportunity for open activity, of course one can see virtue in seeking a refuge and centre of stillness within one's private life as a natural expression of the humanist tradition. This was Montaigne's view during the sixteenth-century wars of religion, repeated in the experience of many dissidents under dictatorships, whether of the right or left. But the weight of humanist opinion has been in favour of an active life, of seeking to master fortune and of resistance rather than resignation in the face of evil.

The issue is graphically illustrated in the twentieth century by the career of Thomas Mann (1875–1955). In the First World War, Mann rejected what he regarded as the Western Allies' ranting about freedom and democracy in favour of the German tradition of *Bildung*, an inner self-cultivation. In his *Confessions of an Unpolitical Man*, published in 1918, Mann wrote: 'Playing politics makes people coarse, vulgar and stupid. Envy, insolence and rapacity are the lessons it teaches. Only the cultivation of the mind makes men free. Institutions matter little, convictions are all-important.'[27]

By 1923, Mann's attitude had changed. At a meeting held in Munich in memory of Walther Rathenau, the Jewish foreign minister of the Weimar Republic who had been assassinated by nationalist thugs, he again spoke of a self-perfection which kept aloof from politics: 'The shaping, deepening and perfecting of one's own life . . . subjectivism in the things of the mind, a life of culture . . . in which the world of the objective, the political world is felt to be profane and is thrust aside. . . .'[28] But this time Mann repudiated such an attitude, calling it a distortion of what Goethe and Humboldt had meant by *Bildung* and *Humanität*. Ten years later, in February 1933, in reaction to the violent right-wing attacks on the Weimar Republic culminating in Hitler's takeover of power, he declared that it was dishonest

To look down scornfully on the political and social sphere and to consider it of secondary importance compared with the world of the inward . . . The political and social is one object of the humane. The interest and passion for humanity, self-dedication to the problem of man . . . are concerned with both aspects, that of the personal and inward and also that of the external arrangement of human life in society.'[29]

In exile in the U.S.A., Thomas Mann became the intellectual leader of the German émigrés and the spokesman of a humanism of which social and political action were an integral part. 'Many of Germany's calamities', he declared (1937), 'have resulted from the mistaken notion that it was possible to be a cultivated, unpolitical man.'

8

Ever since the Greeks recognized the power of critical reason, the power of systematic thought, the place of reason in the humanist tradition has been both central and controversial. Indeed, the history of humanism can be seen as a perennial debate, not about the meaning of the word, but about the scope and claims made for reason.

To the prophets of the Enlightenment, reason was the great liberating force with which to attack all the obstacles and prohibitions inherited from the past that stood in the way of men developing their inherent powers. In my second lecture, however, I quoted from Hume ('Reason is and ought only to be the slave of the passions') in support of my view that to describe the eighteenth century as the Age of Reason, *tout court*, is misleading, and that men as acute and experienced as Voltaire, Diderot,[30] Montesquieu and Adam Smith – as well as Hume – never thought of reason in the absolute terms later rationalists tried to represent. If there was any danger of that, Rousseau provided a powerful reminder that men and women are also creatures of emotion who rely far more on their intuitive than on their intellectual faculties, and are more often moved by passion or habit than by logic or calculation. Montaigne would have laughed – what Renaissance man or woman would not? – to be told that any human being needed to be reminded of this.

For the eighteenth-century *philosophes*, reason had originally an instrumental use, to pose awkward questions and reveal the hollowness of orthodox opinions and conventional wisdom. It was only later that it lost its critical, sceptical character and hardened into a dogmatic rationalism.

It was this one-sided development which Goethe as well as Coleridge warned against. To Goethe, the poet who devoted so much of his time to the study of nature, it was the union of all the human faculties – an equal grasp of the objective and subjective worlds – that brought a man or woman to the highest pitch of development. To Coleridge it was the combination of Imagination with Method that formed the true image of Reason.

This unity has been constantly threatened by an excessive reliance on rationalism on the one hand and the consequences of giving way to the destructive forces of the irrational on the other. In the earlier twentieth century, we have seen the struggles of the writers and artists of the transition period of modernism to come to terms with the claims of the irrational and Freud's exploration of the unconscious mind. The next generation was to learn from experience in the middle of the century, as no other generation in modern times had, what comes of abandoning reason in favour of the irrational. Painfully they rediscovered why the Greeks, whose dramatists show how much they knew about the power of the irrational, attached so much importance to the liberating function of what Freud called the feeble but indispensable light of reason.

The debate will never end. Perhaps we understand better than more recent generations the need to strike a balance, but Coleridge's own disordered life, his tragic inability to give full expression to his genius, is a reminder of how difficult it remains even for someone with his insight into the human condition to translate what he saw into practice.

9

To complete my account of the humanist tradition I want to add two controversial issues which are closely related to the debate about reason: first, humanism and religion; then humanism and science.

Voltaire and other eighteenth-century intellectuals made particular use of the critical powers of reason to attack the power of the established Church. In the nineteenth century, who was to control education – Church or state – was a question which provoked bitter passions, passions which were further inflamed on both sides by the adoption of Darwin's views on evolution and positivist claims for the infallibility of science at the expense of religion. Echoes of these old battles are still to be heard in the almost completely secularized civilization of the West in the late twentieth century, and they may be revived in substance if the aggressive temper of fundamentalism grows in strength.

None the less, while accepting that the humanist tradition inherits from the eighteenth and nineteenth centuries a current of anti-Christian feeling as one of its historical characteristics, the claim sometimes made by both secularists and fundamentalists that secularism *represents* humanism is a travesty – as much a travesty as to take fundamentalism to represent religion. Humanist attitudes towards religion in fact cover a much wider spectrum than rationalist hostility to anything which smacks of the supernatural or the mystical.

At one end of the spectrum, I suggest that the limit is set by the incompatibility between the doctrine of man's fall from grace into a state of sin, from which he can only be redeemed by divine intervention, and the humanist belief in man's potential creative powers, the development of which is in his own hands.

This was the ground of the denunciation of humanism by the Reformers, Luther and Calvin, in the sixteenth century, and Erasmus's attempt to create a Christian humanism was swept away in the quarrel. The decline in religious faith in the modern period led to a renewed attack between the wars on humanism and the liberal Christianity influenced by it, in which the leading figure was the Swiss Protestant theologian, Karl Barth (1886–1968). In his *Epistle to the Romans* (1919) Barth sought to reverse the liberal tendency in the Lutheran Church which went back to Schleiermacher. He described God as 'the wholly other', insisting that there is no way from man to God, but a complete discontinuity between man's 'humanized' ideas of God and the reality. God alone can bridge the gap, by divine revelation through Christ, as an act of grace; man cannot win to Him by his own efforts.[31] Barth subsequently modified his views so far as to admit that 'the wholly other' was too exaggerated a description, and that there was a 'humanity of God' which enabled him to reach out to man. But he did not modify his rejection of any attempt to combine Christian beliefs with humanism which (he said) could only result in 'fundamental concessions to the rights and dignities of man'. For liberal Protestantism, Barth wrote, 'the real object of faith is not God in his revelation, but the man who believes in the divine.'[32]

Barth's uncompromising attitude, supported by formidable abilities as a theologian, gave him a great influence, which was increased by the strong stand he took in warning German Protestants against any appeasement of Hitler. His views did not pass unchallenged by other Protestant theologians at the time, but they have the great merit for my purpose of making clear where the line is drawn at one end of the spectrum.

At the other end one may take an early and often reprinted essay of Bertrand Russell's (1872–1970), 'A Free Man's Worship', in which he declares:

That man is the product of causes which had no prevision of the end they were achieving; that his origin, his growth, his hopes and fears, his loves and his beliefs, are but the outcome of accidental collocations of atoms; that no fire, no heroism, no intensity of thought and feelings, can preserve an individual life beyond the grave; that all the labours of the ages, all the devotion, all the inspiration, all the noonday brightness of human genius, are destined to extinction in the vast death of the solar system – all these things, if not quite beyond dispute, are yet so nearly certain, that no philosophy which rejects them can hope to stand.[33]

Russell's conclusion is that man's own ideals are alone worthy of his reverence, and that, in fighting for them, he has to recognize that he is on his own in a universe at best indifferent and often hostile to them.

This has the same clear-cut character as Karl Barth's views, rejecting *in principle* any form of belief in religious experience or a divine agency as a delusion. But between these two dogmatic extremes, there are a variety of ways in which humanism can be naturally combined with religious belief – Christian, Deist, Jewish – as well as with agnosticism. Not only can be, but has been combined historically, from Erasmus's attempt to recover the original teaching of Jesus by applying the methods of humanistic scholarship; through natural as opposed to revealed religion, the eighteenth-century Deists' belief in a supreme being shared in one form or another by Newton and Locke, Voltaire, Kant and Goethe; to Schleiermacher's religion of feeling, independent of dogma. The Neoplatonists' recognition in the fifteenth century of the essential unity of different religious faiths as converging paths to a simple truth was shared by Lessing and Voltaire in the eighteenth. William James's investigation of the varieties of religious experience was combined with a recognition (which he shared with the agnostic George Eliot) of the pragmatic value of religious faith in transforming men's and women's lives even when there was no certainty of its validity. The modernists in both the Catholic and Protestant churches have sought to restate Christian belief in ways compatible with the results of Higher Criticism and the findings of science.

To these I shall add three more examples from our own times:

Reinhold Niebuhr (1892–1971), for more than thirty years professor at the Union Theological Seminary in New York, first attracted my attention by his political views, expressed in his *Moral Man and Immoral Society* (1932). It was written, he said, out of a deep exasperation with 'the liberal culture of modernity'. He sharply questioned the utopian assumptions of liberal and left-wing thinking and showed a grasp of the problem of power which particularly appealed to me as a political historian. To the optimistic view of man, derived from the Enlightenment, Niebuhr opposed the Christian doctrine of sin, the basis of which he found in human pride,

. . . Pride of power in which the human ego assumes its self-sufficiency and self-mastery . . . , does not recognize the contingent and dependent character of its life and believes itself to be the author of its own existence, the judge of its own values, and the master of its own destiny.[34]

Niebuhr saw the tendency to sin as universal in human life, but he rejected Barth's neo-orthodoxy, insisting that man is not irremediably sinful by nature, but sins in freedom. This is the link with humanism denied by Barth. Since he is a free spirit, man is able to transcend his nature and make history. Niebuhr's expectations of what man could accomplish were restrained: 'The saints are tempted to continue to see that grace may abound, while sinners toil and sweat to make human relations a little more tolerable and slightly more just.'[35] For all that,

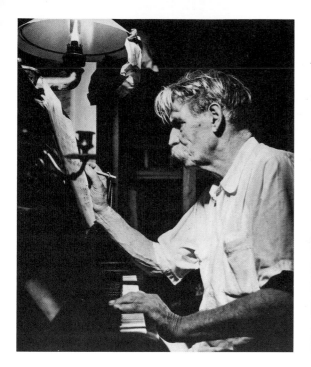
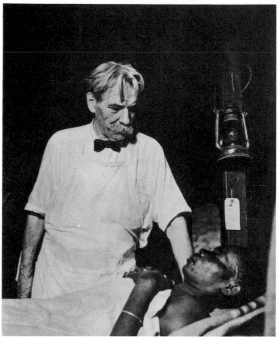

107–8 Two sides of
Schweitzer's life in
Africa in 1955:
practising Bach, and
on his rounds in the
field hospital he built
at Lambarené

Niebuhr was himself active in politics, influenced by Marxism for a
time, a radical critic of the dehumanizing effects of industrial capitalism
(he spent thirteen years as a pastor in Detroit), and a founder (at one time
Chairman) of Americans for Democratic Action. His most impressive
book, the Gifford lectures of 1939 on *The Nature and Destiny of Man*, is an
attempt to combine the insights of the Reformation and the Renaissance
on the basis of his faith in the 'indeterminate possibilities' for man in
history as long as men do not deceive themselves into believing that
absolute solutions of historical problems are within their power.

I should want to include Albert Schweitzer in any case; and his views
happen to form a striking contrast to Niebuhr's Christian realism. Born
in Alsace in 1875, Schweitzer's early career gave proof of outstanding
gifts – in philosophy; in theology (a famous radical work of Biblical
criticism, *The Quest of the Historical Jesus*, 1906, as well as *Paul and his
Interpreters*, and a psychiatric study of Jesus); finally in music, as a concert
organist, co-editor of Bach's organ works and author of a classic study of
Bach. All this had been accomplished by his mid-thirties, but on his
thirtieth birthday (1905) Schweitzer had already decided to devote the
rest of his life to caring for the natives of Equatorial Africa as a
missionary doctor.

Between 1906 and 1913 he qualified as a doctor of medicine at
Strassburg, and in the latter year gave up his academic career to set out
for French Equatorial Africa. In one of the poorest parts of Africa, at
Lambarené, he built and ran a hospital for more than fifty years. His time
was divided between Africa and Europe, where he returned to raise
more money by giving lectures and organ recitals.

Schweitzer maintained that Jesus' teaching and Paul's was dominated by the eschatological beliefs of their age in the imminent end of the world. What retained a universal validity was not the dogmas with which theologians concerned themselves, but Jesus' preaching of the 'ethic of love'. On this Schweitzer built his own philosophy of 'reverence for life' – not just human life, but all living things – believing that it was only by rediscovering this that Western civilization could recover from its sickness.

Schweitzer did not abandon his intellectual interests. He wrote a second book on St Paul, this time on his mysticism; he found a particular affinity with Goethe, and moved out from Christian to religious thought in India, China and other countries. This open-mindedness is expressed in the three volumes of his *Philosophy of Civilisation*, but what made the deepest impression was that a man with his gifts should devote so much of his life to practising what he preached, working as a labourer when his hospital needed rebuilding and treating with his own hands the old, the sick and the poor in one of the most remote corners of the Third World, where he died at the age of ninety in 1965.

Martin Buber (1878–1965) was almost exactly Schweitzer's contemporary, born in Vienna three years after him and dying the same year as he did, in Jerusalem. Buber has had a greater influence on religious thought in the West in this century than any other Jew. In his best known book, *Ich und Du* (1923), he defines the two primary relationships in which man is involved as 'I – It' and 'I – Thou'. The first, which he calls 'experience', describes the objective-functional dimension of human life, those activities which have some *thing* for their object: preserving, doing, thinking, imagining something. These are essential to man, but if anyone were to live only on this level he would be less than a man. The 'I – Thou' attitude, which he describes as 'relation' or 'encounter', is a relation not of subject to object but of subject to subject. Unlike the 'I – It', 'I – Thou' is both a relation of the whole person and one which involves a mutual response absent in the detached, objective attitude of experience. The most obvious case is the relation between two people, but Buber believes it is also possible to have an 'I – Thou' relationship with nature.

Science takes the 'I – It' attitude and shows us a world of objects; religion takes the various 'I – Thou' relationships into which we venture and through these establishes a perspective that leads to the eternal 'Thou' or God. 'Every particular Thou is a glimpse through to the eternal Thou', i.e., the way to God is not through abstract thought or dogma, but through a personal relationship of man to God, of which the human interpersonal relationship of man to man is a reflection.

The ills of the modern world spring from reducing the personal 'I – Thou' relation between men, and between man and God, to an impersonal, subject-object 'I – It' experience, instead of elevating such 'I

– It' attitudes as those towards nature to an 'I – Thou' relationship.

Humanist values seem to me not only compatible with, but an essential part of all three of these very different religious philosophies, Niebuhr's Christian realism, Schweitzer's 'reverence for life', Buber's 'I and Thou'. For my own part I believe that any form of humanism combined with belief in the existence of a power in the universe, greater than oneself, on which one can draw for help, offers a stronger position than one which, to quote Bertrand Russell, sees man as left on his own to sustain those values in an indifferent or hostile universe.

10

In the same book, *Mysticism and Logic*, from which I have already quoted his rejection of religion, Bertrand Russell pins his faith on science as the one sure form of knowledge and the most reliable guide even in the field of moral conduct. This view of science has a long history, reaching back to Lucretius and certain of the pre-Socratic philosophers. Voltaire and the *philosophes* revived it with success in the eighteenth century, acclaiming science as the new revelation which provided the method that would lead to the understanding of man and society, as it already had of the world of nature.

Until the middle of the nineteenth century, science had not developed such a degree of specialization as to make it impossible for educated men to follow the latest discoveries and theories. The division between science and the humanities had not yet taken place. Both Lyell's *Principles of Geology* (1830–33) and Darwin's *Origin of Species* (1859) were widely read and discussed by the general educated public as soon as they appeared.

The break came when science not only became more specialized and professional, but when a distinctive scientific view of man began to be developed. The question then had to be asked, how, following Darwin's demonstration of the continuity of the human species with the rest of the animal kingdom, this was to be reconciled with the traditional views of man held either by religion or by humanism.

The orthodox answer given by T. H. Huxley and repeated by many scientists since is that the scientific view of man, as of the universe, has replaced earlier non-scientific versions, which have now to be discarded in the same way as earlier scientific hypotheses shown by advances in knowledge to have been defective. Taking Comte's three stages of historical development, after the theological and the metaphysical comes the scientific, in which religion and philosophy become redundant, and science emerges as the successor of humanism, the supreme achievement of human reason.

A powerful argument can be made along these lines. The Enlightenment believed that extending the methods of science from the natural to the human realm would liberate men and women. The subsequent success of science has gone a long way to meeting these hopes, not only by raising the standards of human living and material comfort but in relieving human suffering from hunger, pain, disease and fear – immense benefits which we take for granted but which would have seemed miraculous to our predecessors. Science is at the same time the most impressive achievement of the human mind, resting not only on the power of individual genius and the intellectual discipline of the scientific method, but on a cooperative effort which overcomes the obstacles of nationality, culture and language, and puts all other human enterprises in the shade. Surely this is humanism in action.

I do not know how many scientists would take such a view. But it is worth spelling out its implications. Of course many scientists are as much attached to humanist values and as appreciative of the arts and the humanities as those who have had a purely humanistic education. The question is, however, how they see the difference between any insights offered by the arts and the humanities, and scientific knowledge; whether (as Russell did) they regard the latter as alone providing a serious and reliable model for understanding not only the universe but the nature of man and his place in it. For the great success of science has depended on methods which can only be applied to phenomena which are capable of being unambiguously observed and precisely measured. The traditional subject-matter of the arts and the humanities, however – beliefs, values, emotions, the varied response to art, the ambiguities of human experience, and the complexities of social interaction – have not been readily accessible to such methods except on a basis which I see as essentially reductionist and determinist.

I do not think this is altered by the hope which many biologists and physiologists share that, with the great advances already made in the life sciences in this century, it is only a matter of time before the whole of man's life is brought within the scope of scientific explanation and ultimately of scientific control and correction. For what this seems to mean is that the reduction of mental and emotional phenomena to physical causes will then become complete.

I find such a form of explanation unsatisfactory – whether with gaps as at present, or complete – because of the one thing of which I have direct knowledge, as Montaigne long ago pointed out: my own individual experience. That this is dependent upon and indissolubly linked with the physical order both in my own body and in the environment on which I depend for life is undeniable. Nor do I question that the life sciences will continue to throw increasing light on the extraordinarily subtle ways in which this relationship works through genetics and the investigation of the brain. But my experience leads me to believe that human consciousness cannot be reduced to its relationship with the physical vehicle in which it is incarnated, that something else remains – call it what you will, soul, spirit, psyche, mind, stream of consciousness – to be seen as a process rather than as an object, but something which is not reducible to the physical or the social environment on which it depends.

This leads me to the alternative view first elaborated by Vico and developed later by such German thinkers as Dilthey and Cassirer, by Croce and by R. G. Collingwood, that besides the world of nature there is a second dimension in which human beings participate, the world of human culture in the broad anthropological use of that term – of ideas, values, beliefs, the arts, language, symbols, myths, institutions, history (including the history of science) – and that this dimension is distinguished by the fact that men and women, by means of the *Geisteswissenschaften* (translated as the humanities and the social sciences when studied humanistically), can grasp and understand these from the inside – enter into them – because they are human creations.

Let me give a single example of what I mean: a public concert in which a Mozart piano concerto is being played. It is perfectly possible if one mobilizes the different experts – architects, acousticians, physicists, physiologists, experimental psychologists, experts in atmospheric and temperature control, plus economists, sociologists to categorize the performers and audience – to give a complete description of that event down to the last measurable detail. And yet it will not include the one all-important thing that brings all these people together: the experience of playing and listening to Mozart's music, an individual experience different in each case and incapable of being described or measured with any accuracy, but not, I suggest, reducible to the physical conditions on which it is dependent. A change in those physical conditions – for example, my death during the concert – can end the experience, just as death ended Mozart's capacity to produce more concertos. But that does not alter the reality of the experience while I am alive and listening, and what those black marks on the pages of a score can mean to human beings in terms which a scientific explanation of what is taking place, however comprehensive, is inadequate to convey.

Of course the two are complementary. The event and the people involved belong to both worlds – to the physical, and so to be studied by the natural sciences, as well as to the inner world of purpose and meaning to which the *Geisteswissenschaften* give access. Goethe, who valued both equally, the objective and the subjective, insisted on their unity, and I believe that until that unity is recaptured, the humanist tradition will remain the poorer for the alienation from it of perhaps the most impressive of human achievements.

I repeat that I do not know how many scientists would have any sympathy with the view I have been expressing, or with that which I have been attacking. Perhaps the hypothetical scientist with whom I have been arguing is a straw-man; perhaps a scientist in the 1980s would not put the question at all in the way I have, but more in the way Ernst Mach did in the 1880s. How much difference does the twentieth-century revolution in physics make – or the revolution in genetics – or the exploration of the brain? It may be that the explosion of scientific knowledge is proceeding too fast for those who are engaged in it to bother themselves with such questions.

Although they have been regarded with suspicion by many scientists, it is those who have insisted on discussing the philosophical and human implications of science, from A. N. Whitehead to Arthur Koestler, who encourage me to believe that the issues I have been talking about are to be taken seriously. They may well need to be rephrased in quite different terms and language. All I am interested in is in seeing the issues raised, for I am sure I am not alone in believing that this is the greatest of all intellectual challenges, the reconciliation of the two halves of what should be seen as a unity without reducing either to the other.

Nothing would be more exciting than signs of an end to the great schism in Western culture, some movement towards bringing into an intelligible relationship the world as seen by the scientist and the world as seen by the artist, the writer, the critic, the scholar – without sacrificing the independence and validity of either. If that could be achieved, a whole new prospect of human experience would be opened up for the humanist tradition.

Chapter Five
Has Humanism a Future?

It is time to leave the historical development of the humanist tradition, as I have traced it from the Renaissance to the 1930s, and turn in this final lecture to the challenge which it has had to face in the twentieth century. This in turn leads on to the question whether that in effect meant the end of the tradition, or whether humanism still has a role to play in our own times and the future.

For my generation – but not necessarily for a younger generation – the centrepiece of the challenge remains the rise of Nazi Germany, the Second World War, Stalinist Russia and the acute phase of the Cold War – say, from Hitler's accession to power at the beginning of 1933 to Stalin's death in 1953. But in the longer perspective of the century which is available to us in the 1980s, even that series of crises appears as no more than a part of a longer-term set of challenges to the West's tradition of humanism.

It is these that I want to examine now, dividing them into four and bringing the events of 1933–53 into the context of the last of them.

They are:

1. The growth of population and the altered scale of history.
2. Technology and the altered pace of history.
3. Collectivism and the totalitarian state.
4. Wars and the spread of violence.

The total population of the world is estimated to have been 250 million at the time of Christ and risen to 750 million by the beginning of the Industrial Revolution around 1750; it had reached 2,000 million by 1925 and doubled again in the next fifty years. It is expected to reach over 6,000 million by the year 2000. Equally striking is the growth of cities. As late as 1800, there are believed to have been only two cities in the world with a population of more than a million, London and Canton. In 1980 there were 109 cities with a million inhabitants (16 of them over 5 million) and Mexico City is expected to reach 30 millions before the end of the century.

Two consequences, so it is argued, follow from these figures. First, a large proportion of these greatly increased numbers live in conditions of such humiliating poverty, for example in Africa and Latin America, and in cities like Bombay, Mexico City, Djakarta in such degrading conditions of overcrowding, that it becomes a mockery in their case to talk of such things as individual freedom and the other values cherished by the humanist tradition, of anything more than the bare survival of themselves and their children. Second, faced with the size of the problems of providing the bare necessities to keep people alive in the poorer countries of the Third World, or the scale of social organization required to deal with the problems of big cities (even wealthy cities like London or New York) – not only poverty and disease, but crime, exploitation, racial tension, drug abuse – in the face of these, only collective measures based upon aggregates and averages are possible. In such circumstances, who is going to worry, who *can* worry about what happens to individuals?

Science (medicine, for example) and technology (improved health, improved water supplies, improved communications, for example) provide the best means of finding solutions or at least of preventing such problems becoming worse – a fact which those who rail against technology need to remember. But at least for the greater part of this century technological solutions have too often been applied without adequate attention to their appropriateness, to their environmental or their human consequences, and those like E. F. Schumacher (1911–77), who have argued the case for alternative, small-scale or intermediate technologies, for long encountered a wall of prejudice. In the industrialized countries the necessity of allowing nothing to stand in the way of technological advance – particularly doubts raised about the conservation of resources or such long-term consequences for society as putting millions of people out of work or uprooting communities – has become a shibboleth of governments and a new form of the 'iron laws' of classical economics. Even to raise such questions, to ask about comparative costs and benefits or possible alternatives, particularly in regard to military or space technology, is regarded as further evidence of the unsuitability for the technological world of tomorrow of an education which still contains humanistic elements.

For those involved in scientific and technological development there is a breathless sense of excitement at its increasing pace, and the positivist dream of a world transformed by the mastery of nature still has great potency. Nothing can shake their conviction that this must be for the benefit of mankind. But from those who are not active but passive, involuntary participants in the process of change, the individual human beings who make up that convenient abstraction 'mankind', there is a much more ambiguous response. If they recognize the advantages in improved health and standards of living, the message constantly drummed in, that technological advance cannot be stopped or even slowed down and that its consequences simply have to be accepted, produces the conviction that they have no control over developments which can profoundly affect their lives and that as human beings they have ceased to count in the technological scale of values.

The conclusion is easily drawn by the collectivist that the idea of individual human beings having any value or rights is not only an illusion but a highly misleading one, obscuring the fact (according to the argument) that it is only from their membership of a collectivity such as a state, a nation, a race or a social class, that human beings derive either value or rights.

Membership of a group, such as a church, a party, professional or social organizations, has long been one of the rights enjoyed by any individual in a democratic society, and the number and variety of such groups has been regarded as a test of a democracy's strength. Going a stage further, the collectivist idea found expression in trade unionism – 'solidarity is strength', where the individual workman is powerless to defend his interests – and socialist programmes for state or municipal intervention to make provision for the needs (e.g., in education, housing, health) of those who cannot provide for themselves. These were eventually accepted as a natural extension of human rights in an industrialized society.

But there is all the difference in the world between collectivism in this sense and the forms in which twentieth-century collectivism has expressed itself, in integral nationalism, Fascism, Nazism and Communism. In all of these the individual is expected to subordinate his

109 *El Foco* (Focus) by the Spanish artist Juan Genovés (1966) shows humanity as a panic-stricken crowd viewed through the lens of a microscope or caught in the beam of a searchlight

whole life to the demands of an all-inclusive state, intolerant of any suggestion of independence and concentrating all power in its hands, whether this be in the framework of the nation, the *Volk*, the working class, a dominant tribe or a religion such as Islam.

The fact is that the majority of people in the world today live under regimes which, however inefficiently they may operate, are collectivist in character and which regard the human beings under their rule as at their disposal, without any rights which can be asserted against the arbitrary exercise of their power, including imprisonment, torture and death for those who are even suspected of opposing the regime and not infrequently the systematic extermination of ethnic or religious minorities. The confident belief which many liberals and social democrats once held that the pattern of representative government and democratic rights would be extended to the rest of the world outside Western Europe and North America has been shattered. Where the experiment has been attempted, it has all too often collapsed in conditions of corruption and anarchy which have led the population to greet with relief the seizure of power by a strong man or a single party.

Any complacent reflection that this is due to lack of the experience and traditions of the European peoples is immediately checked by recalling that the first Fascist regime to come to power was in Italy, in one of the most civilized nations in Europe, with a humanist tradition going back beyond the Renaissance to Cicero and Republican Rome, and that the two most powerful of all collectivist regimes have both been European – the Nazis' in Germany, which won a greater degree of support than perhaps any other from the most highly educated nation in the world, and the Bolsheviks' in Russia, created in the name of the humanist heresy of Marxism with its roots, however perverted the fruit, in the European Enlightenment.

Fascist Italy and Hitler's Germany were at least frank in their open rejection of the values of Western humanism. The challenge of Soviet Communism was more insidious because it developed a greater internal challenge inside the West than either Fascism or Nazism did.

The Communists claimed that in the Soviet Union they had founded a state which gave more effective expression, on a collectivist basis, to many of the values of the humanist tradition – freedom, the abolition of privilege and the rational organization of society – than was possible in any capitalist society.

Not only did they claim this, but they put more effort into, and had much greater success than the Fascists and their fifth columns, in organizing Communist parties abroad, willing to work under instructions from the Comintern (later the Cominform) in Moscow. This meant that for fifty years (say, between the Bolshevik Revolution of 1917 and the suppression of the 'Prague spring' in 1968) a large section of the working class movements and of the intelligentsia in Western and

110 The individual swallowed up in the collective: Hitler's Nazi Party Rally at Nuremburg, 1934

Central Europe, attracted by the promise of revolution not reform, subordinated their own judgment (often disastrously as in Germany) to the tactics prescribed by the Russians. They did so in the belief that the Soviet Union was a more just, free and equal society than their own and as such had a higher claim on their loyalty. The principal object of Comintern tactics, however, was to eliminate the Communists' rivals in the working class movement, the Social Democrats. The result was to destroy the effectiveness a united movement might have had in securing social and economic reforms, undermine its resistance to Fascism and Nazism and open the way (for example, in Germany and Spain) not to a left-wing revolution, but to the establishment of right-wing dictatorships. It had a subtler but corrosive effect (even when they did not join the Communist Party) on the belief and loyalty of many Western intellectuals to the institutions and humanist traditions of their own countries which they rarely missed an opportunity to denigrate. The brief interlude of a united Popular Front rallying all the progressive forces against Fascism in the late thirties came too late (too late, for example, to save Spain), and was ended by the Nazi–Soviet Pact which Stalin signed with Hitler in 1939.

Revived by the courage with which the Russians defended their country against the Germans, the myth and the illusion still persisted in face of the evidence of the true character of Stalin's rule and the oppressive regimes which the Soviet Union imposed on Eastern Europe and maintained, where necessary, by force. Only in the 1970s did the Western Communist parties, following the Chinese and Yugoslav examples, become sufficiently disillusioned with the Soviet Union to begin to try to work out Marxist programmes in terms of their own national traditions.

While the European left, careless of that humanist tradition from which they derived, remained blinded by the Utopian dream of a left-wing revolution, the real revolutionary innovations of the twentieth century – the techniques of manipulation (the Communist Agitprop and double-talk; Hitler's formula of propaganda plus terror) and the institution of the police state so widely copied since – were first developed in the propaganda ministries, prisons and concentration camps of Soviet Russia and Nazi Germany. Nowhere have they been applied with greater ruthlessness than in the measures Stalin used to break the resistance of the peasants to collectivization, the purges of the 1930s, the creation of the Gulag archipelago. These were matched only by the measures carried out by the Nazi SS in eastern Europe and, most infamous of all, by Hitler's 'Final Solution of the Jewish problem', the systematic extermination of 5–6 million European Jews.

111 Triumph: German troops mark Hitler's subjugation of Greece in 1941 by hoisting the Nazi flag on the Acropolis in Athens, the birthplace of the humanist tradition, within sight of the Parthenon

The experiences which the peoples of Central and Eastern Europe have lived through during the twentieth century (not forgetting the Spanish Civil War or the German occupation of Greece) have no parallel in the history of the continent which has been the matrix of the humanist tradition. A greater proportion of the population, estimated at a third, was wiped out in the Black Death of the fourteenth century; and parts of Central Europe during the Wars of Religion became deserts in which the few survivors were reduced to cannibalism. But it is the scale and the deliberate, systematic character of the destruction of human beings in the twentieth century which stuns the imagination. If one adds up the numbers killed by violence in Europe in the two World Wars, the numbers wiped out in Nazi and Soviet prison camps, the total for the forty years between the outbreak of war in 1914 and Stalin's death in 1953 must be above 50, perhaps 60 million, not to mention the many millions more who, if they survived, did so with bodies which had been mutilated or minds permanently maimed by what had been done to them.

112 Defeat: air view of the destruction in the German city of Hanover at the end of World War II, 1945

175

For a short period from 1924 through 1928, it seemed possible that the cycle of violence and repression which had lasted from 1914 to the end of 1923 might be broken. It was not. The cycle began again with the Great Depression; Stalin's second Russian Revolution (the collectivization of agriculture and the purges); Hitler's rise to power, and the outbreak of the Second World War in 1939. At the end of that war there was no remission: the division of Europe, the Cold War and the threat of a third nuclear war followed straight on. The violence this time spread throughout the world, through Asia, Africa, the Middle East, Latin America, becoming a chronic condition in many parts. The achievement of independence from colonial rule was too often marred by civil war. Racial and communal massacres, deliberately random terrorism as well as assassination, even attempts at genocide, became commonplace.

I do not need to continue this terrible catalogue of inhuman behaviour. It is long enough already, for me to face the question, How can I or anyone else talk about the humanist tradition in the West, as if this still had either validity or relevance in a world as brutalized and indifferent as this has become to values which today only arouse bitterness at the recollection of the hopes they once represented?

2

Before I try to answer that question I need to point out that the account I have given of the twentieth century's history is not complete. It needs to be balanced with other more positive elements. Thus it is a fact that the Western powers not only defeated the external challenges from the Axis Powers and the Soviet bloc, but have done so without abandoning their democratic institutions and values which, however imperfectly, come closest to expressing the humanist tradition. More than that, Western Germany, Italy and Spain have been recovered from Fascism without being lost to Communism.

It is also a fact that the principal ideological challenge to the West, Marxism–Leninism as embodied in the Soviet model and accepted by the other Communist parties, has lost its attractive power, as witness the failure to win over the peoples of Eastern Europe after nearly forty years of Communist rule; the stagnation of the Soviet regime, unable to adapt to change; and the abandonment of the Soviet model by Yugoslavia, China and the Western Marxists.

After the end of the war in 1945, the peoples of Western Europe, including a defeated and divided Germany, staged a remarkable economic and political recovery which, in the twenty-five years between the Marshall Plan and 1973, brought them to a higher level of prosperity, more equally shared, than ever before in their history. Of all the victims of the war none had more cause to be crushed by their

experience than the Jewish survivors of the Holocaust; yet no people showed more resilience or faith than the Jews in the creation of their own state of Israel. The same period saw the end of the colonial empires, in the case of the largest, the British, readily accepted by the British people themselves, who converted what had been a dependent empire into a commonwealth of equals.

The U.S.A., instead of withdrawing abruptly from Europe after the Second World War as it did after the First, undertook the initial responsibility for Europe's economic recovery and for nearly forty years has underwritten the independence of Western Europe through the NATO alliance. In the same period a peaceful revolution has taken place in the position of Black Americans. In the anger which we feel – so rightly feel – at the crimes and evils that remain unrighted, it is important not to forget what has been achieved, if only to encourage ourselves to keep up the struggle to extend it.

Moreover, wherever it is possible to get behind the impersonal forces, the abstractions, the generalizations in terms of which the history of our century is so often presented, wherever it is possible to penetrate to the individual human beings who were involved, one constantly comes across examples of men and women rising to extraordinary heights of courage, self-sacrifice, human sympathy, leadership, endurance – for example, in the Resistance movements, even in the concentration

113 Forty years after the Soviet regime imposed by a Communist government on the Polish people, members of the banned trade union Solidarity continued to defy it. A demonstration at the gates of the Gdansk shipyards in August 1980

114 A member of the French Resistance in World War II faces his German executioners without flinching

camps, and not only in the war but every year since. What is striking about these cases is that they so often describe the behaviour of men and women who found in themselves unsuspected powers to rise above circumstances.

Two questions arise. Why should men and women behave like this, ignoring the risk – in many cases, the certainty – of death or worse, deliberately choosing to place the needs of others, a concept of duty, or loyalty to a cause or ideal, before self-preservation? And why should we admire and applaud them when they do, feeling that their actions, as we say, restore our faith in humanity? This has been the response of most Western peoples throughout history: it has evidently not ceased to be our response now that individual human beings appear so often, to themselves as well as to others, to be reduced to insignificance by the scale and impersonality of events and organizations in the modern world.

This brings me back to the question, how, after the evils inflicted by human beings on others of their own kind, I or anyone else can 'believe in man' or talk about a humanist tradition. If I understand very well the disgust such actions arouse, I in my turn wish to ask, what are the grounds of the disgust, and of the protests which are made – alas, *need* to be made – every day at the inhuman treatment of human beings; what are the grounds of such protests, and for our sense of outrage, other than an instinctive reaction that this is not the way in which human beings should be treated, a belief in the intrinsic value of the individual human being which is the heart of the humanist tradition?

A variant of the counter-argument is that because Nazism and the concentration camps were German phenomena and Germany was the most highly educated, and humanistically educated, of all countries, that fact alone invalidates the humanist tradition. This is an argument put by George Steiner in his lectures *In Bluebeard's Castle*, in which he expresses his revulsion against the humanist tradition of which he himself is a product:

A fair proportion of the intelligentsia and of the institutions of European civilisation met inhumanity with varying degrees of welcome. Nothing in the next door world of Dachau impinged on the great winter cycle of Beethoven's chamber music played in Munich. No canvases came off the museum walls as the butchers strolled reverently past, guide book in hand.[1]

Here I think one has to listen again to Thomas Mann, who saw, and said as early as 1923, that what distinguished the German version of humanism, as this developed after Goethe's and Humboldt's day, from the British, French and American versions was its preoccupation with inner development, *Bildung*, and its rejection of 'the world of the objective, the political world, because, as Luther says, "this external order is of no consequence!"'[2] It was this one-sided concentration on *Innerlichkeit*, from which Mann, like Goethe, had only freed himself with difficulty, that he saw as the explanation of why, so often in Germany history, evil had resulted from good – in the Reformation, in the Romantic Movement, in the failure of the German educated classes to resist Nazism.

I do not suggest that by itself this can explain the rise of Hitler or even the complacency with which the educated classes in Germany watched him come to power. Nazism is not a phenomenon capable of a single explanation. But I believe Mann touches on a very important point for our own time – the distaste and disdain which educated people, whether they have had a humanistic or a scientific education, often feel for politics conducted in the popular style of today's democracies; and the consequences which can follow from their abandonment of the ideal of civic humanism.

The element in the humanist tradition which grates on those who have lived through the twentieth century is that belief in the natural goodness of man and his perfectibility, the optimism which marked the eighteenth-century Enlightenment, the confidence which the nineteenth-century positivist version of humanism felt in science, progress and the future. But this is to make the mistake, to which I have pointed several times, of taking a particular phase in the historical development of humanism as representative of the whole. The Enlightenment is only one such phase in a humanist tradition which goes back to the ancient world and to the rediscovery of that world in the Renaissance.

Neglect of this earlier history of humanism, for example the Stoicism of the ancient world, or its restatement by Montaigne in the middle of the cruelties and intolerance of the Wars of Religion, has led many of its critics to overlook that more realistic humanist view which, accepting the limitations and weaknesses of men and women, puts its faith, not in their natural goodness – any more than their natural wickedness – but in their potential creativity and what that latent power can accomplish once awakened.

As I have shown, this alternative to the optimistic version of the eighteenth century was kept alive by a succession of humanist writers in the nineteenth century from Goethe to Matthew Arnold, Ruskin and Morris, highly critical of those who believed in the inevitability of progress. Between the 1880s and the 1930s, a new version of humanism was beginning to emerge which had broken with the optimistic assumptions of the earlier phase and accepted that its starting-point had to be recognition of the divided nature of man, of the irrational forces in individual human beings and in human society which such pioneers as Ibsen, Freud and Max Weber had made explicit.

No philosophy of man could come through the experience of the mid-twentieth century unscathed. But this is true of the Christian, Marxist and scientific as much as of the humanist view, all of which have had to struggle to come to terms with the depths of human suffering and evil which it revealed. But the humanist tradition which had to face that challenge was something very different from the liberal-optimistic-positivist version which was the image of it left by the nineteenth century. How far the promise of this new version of the tradition could survive the experience and face the continuing challenges I have described is a question I have still to discuss. But the double fact that the treatment of human beings under Hitler's and Stalin's regimes produced an unequalled sense of outrage, and secondly that those who recovered their freedom after the war, whether in Western Europe or Israel, showed unequalled powers of resilience suggests that the question is not to be dismissed out of hand.

3

An argument of a different kind is that humanism is an ideology which belongs to the period of bourgeois individualism and has no place in a world which has moved from individualism to collectivism.

The value of the historical approach which I have followed is that it shows an identification of humanism with bourgeois individualism in the Marxist sense to be applicable only to a particular phase in its history, say the century and a half that separates Adam Smith's *Wealth of Nations* (1776) from the publication of Keynes's *General Theory of Employment Interest and Money* in the mid-1930s and Roosevelt's New Deal. It is an unconvincing description of the original humanism of the ancient world or of the Renaissance in which it was reborn. And it ignores the alternative version of humanism critical of precisely those elements most obviously identifiable with economic individualism which was never without representation in the nineteenth century, and which at the end of the nineteenth and the beginning of the twentieth century bore fruit in the adoption of interventionist programmes by liberal and social democratic parties.

Except within those historical limits, I see no reason to accept the glib identification of economic individualism with the much more fundamental sense of human individuality which, I agree, is central to the humanist tradition. Individuality, however, does not imply an atomic view of society as made up of individuals who are shut in upon themselves in suspicious and hostile isolation. On the contrary, in the humanist view the social impulses, the desire to develop human relationships, the need for affection and for cooperation, the need to belong to human groups, are an essential part of human life without which the identity of the individual remains stunted.

Combination for action with others is one of the greatest potential assets of human beings, perhaps their greatest. Membership of a group, whether voluntary or, as in the case of a nation or an ethnic culture, something one is born into, is a necessary and deeply satisfying expression of human individuality. Man is a social being as well as a separately identifiable individual.

Clever men in our time have argued that the Death of God has been followed by the Death of Man; that the identity of the self and individual consciousness have been dissolved into no more than a succession of unconnected sensations. This is a view discussed by David Hume two centuries ago, and by William James in his *Principles of Psychology*, without being accepted by either. Others have argued that, since individual human beings are conditioned by their class or social environment, such words as freedom, responsibility, justice, humanity, either mean nothing or have meaning only when applied to such collectivities as a class, a nation or a race.

Nobody can ignore the necessity in the twentieth century for collective action – by trade unions, political parties, pressure groups and the state – if men and women are to secure and depend on their liberties or rights. Nor, as I have said, can I see any inconsistency between this necessity and the emphasis of the humanist tradition on human individuality; on the contrary, I see such action as an extension and protection of it. But it is my belief that the great majority of human beings, in Western countries at least, whatever their political affiliations, continue to think of themselves, and believe they have rights and should be valued, as individuals. It is equally my belief that, far from being either eradicated or satisfied, it is this sense of individual identity to which those who have suffered or still suffer under the collectivist regimes of Central and Eastern Europe cling most strongly. Osip

Mandelstam (1891–1938), the Russian poet who perished in one of Stalin's prison camps, wrote that the measure of the social structure is man, but that there are eras in which this is lost sight of, when 'people say they have no time for man and that he is to be used like bricks or cement as something to be built *from* not *for*.' Mandelstam compared the Stalinist regime under which he lived to those of the ancient Assyrian and Egyptian kings. His widow, Nadezhda, added in her unequalled account of life in Soviet Russia:

And what difference is there between those prisoners destroyed on the orders of Assyrian kings and the 'masses' which now inspire us with such awe, always appearing whenever an 'iron' social order is established? Yet in their everyday working lives people remain true to their individual selves. I have always been struck by the fact that in the closed world of a hospital, factory or theatre, people live their own completely human lives, not becoming mechanized or turning into 'masses'.[3]

Nadezhda Mandelstam's remark about 'the masses' at once raises the question of the world outside Europe and North America, the teeming, impoverished world of Africa, Asia, South and Central America. What validity or relevance has the humanist tradition of the West for them?

One of the criticisms made of these lectures by Indian and other Asian friends is that I have assumed the humanist tradition is peculiar to the West, and that there is nothing corresponding to it in, for example,

115 Mahatma Gandhi, leader of the campaign of non-violent resistance against the British in India

Indian or Chinese culture. This is a just criticism. Even if the limitations of my experience make it impossible for me to bring these different traditions into the account I am giving of the Western tradition, it is important at least to acknowledge the existence of other humanist traditions elsewhere. One example must suffice to suggest how much the West may have to learn from them.

Of those leaders who have succeeded in the twentieth century in galvanizing 'the masses' into action, none has spoken a language which ought to be more easily understood by the West than Gandhi (1869–1948), whose reading of Tolstoy and Thoreau helped him to formulate the strategy of civil disobedience and passive resistance which in the end defeated the British.

After independence had been won, Gandhi's action in going to Calcutta, the scene of some of the worst communal riots, and risking his life and his authority in appealing to both Hindus and Moslems to stop the massacres, is an outstanding example of that civil courage which is a part of the humanist tradition. No less striking is the answer he gave when those who were closest to him asked what talisman he would leave with them for the time when they had to assume the task of governing India without him. Gandhi replied that, whenever they were about to make a decision, each of them should think of the poorest man they had ever met and ask themselves what benefit the decision would bring to him.[4]

The history of the twentieth century looks very different when it is seen from the angle of Asia and the Third World. It is dominated by the end of colonialism, independence, and if not revolution as well, at least the beginning of that process of modernization which disrupts traditional societies. From the Asians and Africans I have known, I believe that, as this process continues, at least in the more fortunate parts of the non-Western world, and as soon as the inhabitants are able to raise their eyes above survival, the idea of human rights, whether or not this is already a part of their own traditions (limited to a particular caste or class), will be among the first which they grasp and seek to make their own.

It will be a very long time, if ever, before human rights can become a reality for the hundreds, even thousands, of millions for whom at present it means nothing. But that is not the end of the matter. Even if that is true, two things are of great importance. The first is that the idea should not be ruled out, in principle, as inapplicable to those who live in the Third World, even if it can only be applied to particular invidividual cases as a start. The second is that in our own dealings with those parts of the world we have to remain true to the philosophy which has produced our institutions, we have to insist that we do not ourselves accept *apartheid*, the exclusion of those of different race and culture from consideration as human beings entitled to the same rights as ourselves.

116 A demonstration by Argentine wives in August 1983 on behalf of the thousands who had 'disappeared' without trace or trial under the military dictatorship – which has since been removed from office

I do not believe that those who suffer under Latin American or African dictatorships (whether white or black) fail to understand the appeals and protests made on their behalf in the name of human rights. The U.N. Charter and the European Convention on Human Rights, and the operations of Amnesty International, may still be frail instruments in a violent world, but they represent a first attempt to extend to all countries the rights which are protected in our own by the constitution and the law, and they have a surprising impact even in countries living under dictatorship, whether of the right or the left. No one will convince me that the humanistic concept of such rights is anachronistic, irrelevant, bourgeois, white suprematist or neo-imperialist.

4

It is still, however, in relation to the Western world that the question of relevance has first to be answered. For if we, with our higher standards of living, and well-established institutions, such as representative assemblies, responsible government, free elections, the rule of law, civil peace, public education, freedom of opinion, the welfare state – all of which derive from the humanist tradition – if we who owe so much to that tradition have lost faith in its relevance, the rest of the world is not likely to be convinced.

Until they are threatened or lost, such institutions, once established, are easily taken for granted and attention concentrated on their shortcomings in practice rather than the achievement they represent. But the case for the relevance of the humanist tradition rests not on the continued value of what it has bequeathed to our societies – although I think it important to recognize that – but on its capacity for developing answers to the new problems which beset them.

What problems? Instead of repeating a list that anyone can compile from reading a single issue of a newspaper like the *New York Times* or *The Guardian* – inner city decay, drugs, dropouts, vandalism, crime, violence, the breakup of the family, child abuse, unemployment, poverty, racial tension, terrorism, the loneliness of the old, pollution, the arms race, fear of a nuclear war – instead of elaborating that litany of human misery, let me make two general points.

The first is that we are imperfect creatures living in an imperfect world. Nobody is going to get rid of their problems for good even in the most prosperous and advanced societies. But there is a limit to the amount of human misery and anger that a society can tolerate. Beyond a certain point, of course, it can lead to a breakdown of civil order, to 'no go' areas, even to the threat of revolution and civil war. But that is not a situation likely to occur in the organized industrialized countries of Western Europe and North America except as a result of war and defeat, although I believe that fear of it and the measures taken to prevent it can intensify the real danger. But I see the real threat, not in revolution and street fighting, but in a growing deterioration, already taking place, in human relations, in the way people treat each other, which is the substance behind the abstract term society. I have in mind the private world of the family, the personal relations between men and women, the treatment of children and the old, *and* the public world of politics, local, and national, even international relations, the school and community, including relations in the workplace. If I have to find a word to describe what I fear it is an autistic society, a world in which men and women shut themselves up in their own private worlds and become so afraid of communicating with each other that they lose the habit of it.

The second point I want to make is that while this deterioration hits the poor and the disadvantaged hardest, no one is exempt from its effects any more. As the prosperous classes discovered in the nineteenth century, no one is exempt from a cholera epidemic – a discovery which led to effective public health measures being taken. The strength of any society lies not only in the factors which can be measured in economic and social statistics, but in its cohesion, its moral fibre, the existence of sufficient sense of common interest, common values and trust among its members to meet a challenge without falling apart into quarrelling groups such as broke up German society after 1918, thus opening the way to Hitler, or a general *sauve qui peut* such as defeated the French in 1940.

If we are not prepared to accept a Hobbesian view of the future of human society as dominated by power and fear – Hitler's view, and Stalin's – I believe that the humanistic approach has an indispensable contribution to make to the ways in which we can hope, if not to eliminate, at least to alleviate our problems. Many of them are not accessible to government intervention, and even when they are, this is all too often ineffective (as overseas aid is) unless it can build upon initiatives from below – or at least a response at the grass roots.

Of all the beliefs with which the humanist tradition has been identified from its rebirth in the Renaissance it is that men are not powerless in the face of fortune but have within them creative energies which, once they can be released, make it possible for them to master their situation. During the student troubles in the late 1960s and 1970s when I was the head of a university, I had to fight hard against becoming infected with a siege mentality, and alienated from the young. What first gave me confidence that the humanist belief was still relevant was becoming involved with my wife and Jessie Emmet (after whom these lectures are named) in an Aspen programme, to which we gave the title *The First Twenty Years of Life*. We had in mind to explore the problems created, and encountered, by young people, from the effect on children of the breakup of families by divorce to teenage pregnancy and youth unemployment. It was from this programme that I learned how much young people and those dedicated men and women who seek to help them were already turning to self-help, individually and in support groups, to cope with the disconcerting world in which they were growing up.

I had the same experience with students in my own country. As a result, I have learned, in a world in which older people are continually deploring the disappearance of values, the extent to which young people are trying to work out for themselves new values to live by, their own codes of behaviour, their own concepts of conscience and of the qualities they prize. They are not the same as those of their grandparents, but neither were ours the same as the values of the Victorian age, nor the Victorians' as those of the eighteenth century.

I suspect that this is the only way in which values can be re-created in the modern world, no longer by direct transmission but by encouraging young people to discover, or rediscover, them for themselves, out of their own experience and insights, often in discussion with their peers, not taken on authority but deeply influenced by the sympathy and above all the example (practice not precept) of older people.

At a time when the place of the humanities in education is under question, young people's search for values by which to live seems to me to define the role the humanities can play. It will require something of a revolution in the presentation of history, literature and the arts, to start not from the achievements of the past, but from the human needs of young people today. But it is the same role which the rediscovery of the ancient world played for the Renaissance, providing those who were young then with a strange and exciting world which they could explore and on which they could draw to work out their own answers to the questions and conflicts presented by their own experience. Today the material on which to draw is no longer limited to the ancient world, but includes the whole range of human experience, contemporary as well as historical, that of other cultures as well as our own Western tradition. This material, thanks to film, television and videos, is now accessible as never before.

Here is a great opportunity to make available to young people in schools and colleges, not a traditional course in the humanities, but a direct encounter, taking advantage of these new media, with human experience of the questions that bother and fascinate them. It could focus in turn on such questions as conscience, conflicts of loyalty, rebellion and authority, the ambivalence of feelings, the search for identity, the power of art and myth, passions and compassion, as these are reflected in literature, theatre, the arts, history and philosophical debate – with the same object, to prompt them, as the discovery of Greece and Rome prompted the young people of the Renaissance, to reach their own conclusions.

Any such encounter with the humanities is valuable not only for the results it can produce, but for the activity itself, engaging the imagination and the emotions in the penetration of other people's worlds and ideas. In an education which is all too inclined to fill students with information and limit itself to teaching them techniques, here is a way of fostering the emotional, subjective side of human nature which is of so much importance for young people, and which needs to be developed as much as the intellectual if they are to acquire confidence and establish satisfying relationships with other human beings.

5

I have concentrated on the needs of young people because these are both the most vulnerable and the most hopeful. But all of us are confronted with change and at times feel bewildered. I have been struck by the extent to which those women who are seeking to define new roles for themselves have turned to search out the experience of other women in the past, through women's writing, journals, letters, the history of the family and of the struggle for women's rights, making use of that power which the humanities give to recover and bring back to life what other women have created.

It is because the humanities and the arts directly and uniquely address themselves to the human condition, because they respond to and can help to meet that hunger for individual identity, for a meaning for individual lives, which is certainly not less a feature of our times now than in the past, that I believe they ought to remain an essential part of our education and lives.

Will this argument no longer be valid in the world of the future? My belief is that it may even gain in force, whichever hypothesis you incline to about the future: the optimistic one that the world of the future will give us more leisure and freedom than we know what to do with; or the pessimistic one that the conditions of modern life will press more restrictions upon us, as if we were condemned to live forever in crowded airports. I suggest that whichever is nearer the truth – whether from a sense of new possibilities or in defence of a humanity they feel threatened – men and women are going to need and claim more, not less, insistently than in the past the opportunity to develop their individuality, establish their identity and be treated as people in their own right, not as the objects of social or the instruments of political policy.

I can find plenty of evidence in support of that view in the protest movements which have become a feature of Western societies today. As an elderly, middle-class private citizen, I am as irritated as the next man by the exaggeration, aggressiveness and exhibitionism which they frequently express. But as an historian I can see – from my knowledge of what such protest movements, equally noisy and disturbing, have accomplished in the past – that they are also the expression of something central to both the humanist tradition and democratic institutions. This

117 Votes for Women. A demonstration in London in June 1910 by members of the Women's Social and Political Union

was the element the lack of which Thomas Mann saw as fatal to the German tradition of *Humanität*. I mean the refusal to accept without question the wisdom of governments, to turn a blind eye to abuses and injustice, and above all the refusal to acquiesce in the fatalistic argument that nothing can be done to change things, that ordinary people cannot make their voices heard.

The example I have already mentioned, women's changing perceptions of their roles, illustrates my argument. Nothing has roused my anger more in my historical explorations than the frustration of women who felt themselves – often with far more justification than men – to be the heirs and transmitters of the humanist tradition and yet were denied recognition of this by prejudice, including the right to contribute to it openly. Charlotte (1816–55) and Emily Brontë (1818–48), today seen as among the greatest English writers of the nineteenth century, like George Eliot, could only publish under assumed men's names as Currer and Ellis Bell; Emily Dickinson (1830–86) was so constrained by the conventions of her time that she published only seven poems in all, leaving unpublished more than 1750 others which have since established her as a great lyric poet.

To describe the belated efforts now being made to do justice to the unacknowledged contribution women have made is not 'feminism'. Ibsen was right when he said it was a question not of women's but of human rights. The movement for greater equality between men and women has been attacked in recent years as strident, unbalanced, egotistical, destructive of the family – and all the other epithets that were applied to the agitation for women's votes earlier in the century; but to me there is no question that, however painful and protracted the process of change may be, the humanist tradition will be turned into a mockery if the balance between the sexes is not made more equal.

No one has ever expressed the case for protest more cogently than Martin Luther King (1929–68) in his letter from Birmingham Jail, Alabama, written to his fellow ministers in the city at the height of the Civil Rights Movement in 1963.

You may well ask [he wrote], 'Why direct action? Why sit-ins, marches, etc.? Isn't negotiation a better path? You are exactly right in your call for negotiation. Indeed this is the purpose of direct action. Non-violent direct action seeks to create such a crisis and establish such creative tension that a community that has constantly refused to negotiate is forced to confront the issue. It seeks so to dramatise the issue that it can no longer be ignored. . . . My friends, I must say to you that we have not made a single gain in civil rights without determined legal and non-violent pressure. History is the long and tragic story of the fact that privileged groups seldom give up their privileges voluntarily. . . .

Quoting St Augustine and St Thomas Aquinas in his support, King argues that there is a distinction between just and unjust laws.

118 Martin Luther King during his campaign for civil rights and against racial discrimination

I would agree with St Augustine that 'An unjust law is no law at all' . . . It gives the segregator a false sense of superiority, and the segregated a false sense of inferiority. To use the words of Martin Buber, the great Jewish philosopher, segregation substitutes an 'I–It' relationship for the 'I–Thou' relationship, and ends up relegating persons to the status of things.[5]

In any anthology of twentieth-century humanism, the Letter from a Birmingham Jail would be high on my list of documents that cannot be left out.

6

I do not believe that humanism can be *identified* with protest any more than religion can be *identified* with liberation theology. That would be to give too narrow a basis to what is a continuous and wide-ranging debate about the nature and destiny of man. In my last lecture you will recall how much I made of the shift in consciousness and in the way men and women came to see themselves as the key to what Brandes called 'the modern breakthrough' as early as 1882, thirty years before the actual breakup of the existing European order in the First World War. At that juncture in its history, it was more important than anything else for the humanist tradition to adapt itself to recognition of the irrational in human behaviour and the other elements which go to make up the change in consciousness from the nineteenth to the twentieth century.

One way of ending these lectures would have been to take up the promise of a new version of humanism created by the writers and thinkers, the scientists and the artists of the 'modern period' in the first half of this century and see how far it has been completed by Heidegger, Lévi Strauss, the structuralists and comparative grammarians who, George Steiner claims, are the 'evident heirs to the Renaissance and the Enlightenment.'[6] If I have chosen to concentrate instead on the prospects of a new version of humanism being translated into action in the same way as the Enlightenment version in the late eighteenth and nineteenth centuries, it is because I believe that the future of humanism now depends more upon this than on the originality and truth of what is written, said and created in the private worlds of writers and artists, philosophers and critics. Until such a prospect can be opened, the isolation of these private worlds from the everyday world of the late twentieth century in which we all live and the consequent frustration, will remain as complete as it is now.

I have already suggested one way in which an opening may be created, by making clear that the permanent values of the humanist tradition, freedom, equality and human rights, apply and should be extended to those who hitherto have been – and resent being – excluded from a share in them.

But protest, though it is an essential part of the action necessary to validate humanist principles in today's world, is only a part of it. By definition it is the action, the *only* action open to them, of people excluded from the power to make decisions. But what about those who have that power? Has humanism nothing to contribute, other than protest, to the world of politics, government and business?

Some years ago, J. E. Slater, the President of the Aspen Institute, persuaded it to set up a programme on governance, which he defined as the problems presented by the inadequacy of our institutions, especially public but also corporate, national as well as international, to cope with societies which threaten to become ungovernable.

It did not take long to discover that at least one of the reasons for the growth of ungovernability lies in the widespread scepticism of those on the outside about the chances of ever getting any large organization to respond to their needs or to criticism, unless it is possible to mount large-scale protests. But those on the inside also include men who are deeply disturbed by the gap not only of credibility but of authority which they see opening between them and the public, and who are frustrated by the inertia of big organizations, the vested interests of the hierarchies, the entrenched tradition of specialization.

In very different ways both Kafka and Max Weber foresaw the growth of this problem of bureaucracy, a problem which is common alike to Western, Communist and Third World societies. It was, after all, the Prague rebels of 1968 who coined the slogan 'Socialism with a human face'. The attempt to find a way of achieving that has attracted a number of Marxist theoreticians of whom Habermas (1929–) and the Frankfurt School, and the Italian Communist leader Gramsci (1891–1937) are the most interesting. But the need to reconcile a humanist Marxism (the phrase is now in common use) with the Procrustian bed of Marxist dogmatism presents an additional obstacle from which the West is free. Here, at least in principle, reform ought to be easier for an active form of civic humanism.

Let me add one final portrait to my gallery of humanists to illustrate my argument.

John Maynard Keynes (1883–1946) has had the greatest impact on public affairs of any economist since Adam Smith, Ricardo and Marx. But until his thirties, he gave little indication that he would play any such role. At Cambridge, where he read mathematics, he became a member of a coterie much under the influence of the philosophy of G. E. Moore (1873–1958). Moore's teaching promoted a kind of moral narcissism with the doctrine that morality is a matter of states of mind rather than actions, and that affectionate personal relations and the contemplation of beauty are the only supremely good states of mind. Such views, which are not all that different from those of the circle that surrounded Lorenzo de Medici in Florence, encouraged the conclusion that the most desirable life was one lived on intimate terms with one's friends (Keynes was an active homosexual) in the pursuit of truth and beauty, free of all external obligations and insulated against the ambitions and values of ordinary folk, which were immoral because they were ugly and distasteful.

Keynes found all that he needed in the intense closed society in which he lived as a Fellow of King's College, Cambridge and the Bloomsbury group in London – and he might well have continued to do so if it had not been for the impact of the First World War. Drafted into the Treasury, his anger at the way the post-war negotiations with the Germans were conducted led him to publish, at the age of thirty-seven, a brilliant and polemical attack on *The Economic Consequences of the Peace* (1919).[7] From this eruption into public life he never looked back, going on not only to revolutionize economic theory but to take active steps to get his ideas put into practice, providing the economic programme for Lloyd George's 1929 election campaign ('We Can Conquer Unemployment', the first political pamphlet I ever bought at the age of 15); converting the British Treasury with his pamphlet 'How to Pay for the War'; playing a leading role at Bretton Woods in setting up the post-war international monetary system and negotiating the U.S. loan to Britain. On the side he wrote some of the best political journalism of the century, made a fortune on the Stock Exchange for himself and another for his college, and was both a connoisseur and patron of the arts. Keynes

119 John Maynard
Keynes in his mid-
twenties, painted by
Gwen Raverat in 1908

is a modern version of *l'uomo universale* admired by the Renaissance
Italians, whose eventual commitment to an active civic humanism
meant that his ideas and energies reached out to benefit not only his own
country but the whole Western world.

The lesson of Keynes's success is that, however many ideas for reform
are generated outside the system, they will only make an impact if those
within it can be engaged in dialogue and persuaded of the need for
change. One way of doing this is that pioneered by the Aspen Institute in
bringing together government and business executives, politicians,
judges, academics, and private citizens to discuss the problems of our
societies as individual human beings in situations where no one is any
longer protected by his or her professional armour, no longer allowed to
confine themselves to the rut of their unchallenged assumptions. As one
example of many, I recall an Aspen 'Corporation and Society' seminar,
bringing together half a dozen heads of big corporations with some of
the young lawyers who worked for consumer and other public interest
groups, and the impact (on both sides) of moving from formal
confrontation to informal face-to-face discussion.

Another key point of entry is in professional education. I question the
assumptions that are hidden in that word 'professional': the comfortable
narrowing of responsibilities which it so often implies ('the operation
was a great success; too bad the patient died'). It is at the point where
professional attitudes are being formed that an effort needs to be made to
bring home the balance of professional competence with understanding
of human problems and values. Limiting the professional's liability for
damages is not enough.

Libraries have been filled with proposals for such reforms. Among them a modest place is occupied by the Bullock Report on Industrial Democracy (1977),[8] the experience of producing which taught me something of the strength of resistance to change even when we could point to the successful application, in such countries as Germany, Austria and Sweden, of our proposals for worker participation on the boards of large private and public enterprises. But the experience of producing that report also left me with a firmer belief in the relevance of a humanist critique to these problems of governance. Here are a few of the insights which I believe such a critique can highlight and which are too often neglected.

First, the whole history of the twentieth century in Russia and China as much as the West is there to warn that the attempt to limit oneself to finding technical solutions to technical problems, however attractive, is an illusion. The human dimension cannot be left out. How to overcome resistance to innovation, how to win cooperation: these are the most difficult, and in the end the decisive questions.

Second, while the computer and modern communications systems are marvellous aids to human decision-making and the exercise of leadership, they are not a substitute for them, not a way by which those with a responsibility to decide and lead can escape from making judgments, which inevitably include value judgments. There is no escape into an impersonal world of automatic responses to standard questions.

The third is that the greatest resources available to any organization are the human ingenuity, experience and loyalty it can draw on. None are more commonly undervalued. Yet any investment put into tapping these by education (education far more than training), by securing active participation and with it the commitment of those working in any enterprise to its success will produce greater returns than piling up investment in sites, buildings and equipment.

Fourth, nothing can have a more searching effect than to apply to the cumbersome organizations and programmes of the twentieth century the questions Bentham and the philosophical radicals applied to those of the *ancien régime*:

What is the use of this?

What purpose does it serve?

Is it necessary? Does it serve the people it is supposed to serve?

Do they want something else?

Can their demands be met more simply?

7

Now, if you ask me whether I suppose that in a world as ossified in its structures as ours I expect that the statement of the obvious in the pure light of reason is going to produce any effect, I have to answer 'No'. I would press hard to see such a humanist critique made part of managerial and professorial education, but *by itself* I do not expect this to make any real difference. After all, even the far more drastic methods of Mao's cultural revolution only succeeded in cowing, not uprooting, the Chinese bureaucracy. I might well despair were it not for my belief in what Hegel called 'the cunning of history', a grandiose phrase for the inevitability of change and the unavoidability, even for bureaucracies, of having to adapt to it.

Who, even twenty years ago, would have believed how much the progress of technology would change the great concentrations of heavy manufacturing with which industry was then still identified? Why should we assume that the large-scale bureaucratic organizations characteristic of today – both in government and in the corporate sector – will be exempt from similar change, or that the progress of technology can only lead to larger and larger concentrations of power? Could it be that technology may make possible smaller-scale, decentralized organizations, and so turn out to be on the side of the individual and the small groups in which the individual feels at home, instead of strengthening the faceless, all-pervasive impersonal power which George Orwell made the nightmare of 1984? Is that an option open to us, and if so, what are we doing to explore it? The question is at least worth asking, like that other question which we have made the subject of an Aspen Institute study, What will changes in the pattern of work mean, not just for production, for economics, but for human beings, for their education, their ways of living and finding satisfaction?

If I ask myself what conclusion I draw from a lifetime spent in the study of history and the humanities, I would put it into five words: the future is not predictable. Who knows what the agenda for tomorrow will turn out to be? Some things *are* predictable, particularly those which can be measured, some at least of the discoveries that will be made, including the progress of technology. But even if you can go a long way towards predicting the external circumstances in which men and women will be living in fifty or a hundred years from now, what no one can predict is how they will react to them. If you go back and look at what was foreseen at the beginning of this century, you will find that man's flight to the moon was correctly predicted, but not the course of human history, not what men and women would make of the world in which we now live.

How many foresaw the length and character of the 1914 war; foresaw that Germany would lose it or, having lost it, would make a second bid for European hegemony?

How many foresaw that Hitler and the Nazis would come to power; that the 1000-year Reich would last only twelve years; that Hitler, who appeared irresistible in 1940, would lead Germany to defeat a second

time, but before doing so would attempt to wipe out the Jewish
population of Europe?

How many foresaw that from the Holocaust the state of Israel would
be born; that the European empires – including the British – would not
survive the war; that Japan, re-created with American aid, would
become the U.S.A.'s chief technological and economic rival, and that a
twice defeated and divided Germany would finally emerge as the victor
of the Anglo–German encounter?

So I could go on. Who at the end of the eighteenth century foresaw
what vast changes industrialization, at that time represented by a few
textile factories and iron forges in Britain, would lead to? Who at the
end of the nineteenth century foresaw the revolution in physics which
was to transform the scientists' view of the universe and matter?

It is the study of history and the humanities that keeps alive our sense of a future which is still open. This was what happened when, quite unpredictably, in fourteenth-century Italy, a handful of men felt the impulse to recover the world of antiquity and from that derived the confidence to create a new world of their own.

This is what, throughout these 600 years, the humanist tradition has represented, a refusal to accept a determinist or a reductionist view of man, an insistence that in some measure men and women, if they do not enjoy complete freedom, none the less have it in their hands to make choices.

For those who crave for security, for a guarantee that, if they commit themselves, the desired results will follow, this is not enough. But for those who accept that faith has always been a matter of the leap of commitment before the evidence is complete, and who rebel against the sense of impotence with which we are pressed down, I submit that this is the continuing attraction of the humanist approach. It does not guarantee that men and women will make good choices, correctly foresee the results or escape disaster – only that there are still choices to be made, if we can find the courage and the will to make them.

121 The latest phase of the industrial revolution. Robots in place of welders on the assembly line at the Ford Motor Company's body plant, Dagenham, London, in 1982

197

Notes and References

Introduction and Chapter I
The Renaissance

1 Among the musicians were Arthur Rubinstein, Gregor Piatigorsky, and the Minneapolis Symphony Orchestra under Dimitri Mitropoulos. From this side of the Goethe celebrations stems the annual Aspen Music Festival.

2 Cicero, *De Oratore* (55 BC); Quintilian, *Institutio Oratoria (c.* AD 96).

3 Erwin Panofsky, *Renaissance and Renascences in Western Art* (Stockholm 1960, New York 1969), ch. 1 and 2.

4 Francesco Petrarca, *Prose (La Letteratura Italiana, Storia e Testi,* v. 7, Milan 1955), *De Sui ipsius et multorum ignorantia liber,* Latin text with Ital. transl., pp. 722–23.

5 My colleague, Dr George Holmes, who is an authority on the Italian Renaissance, has pointed out to me the importance of the notaries among the educated laymen. There were 600 of them in Florence alone in the mid-fourteenth century. They were closely connected with lawyers and dominated the production of documents, both private conveyances and the official documents of the many chanceries. Nearly all the principal humanists, from Petrarch, Bruni and Salutati to Machiavelli, were either notaries themselves or came from the families of notaries with a professional interest in writing first-class Latin. I am indebted to Dr Holmes for this and for a number of other expert comments on this chapter.

6 Peter Burke, *Culture and Society in Renaissance Europe, 1420–1540* (London 1972), ch. 9, 'The Social Framework'.

7 Burke, *op. cit.,* Appendix, 'The Creative Elite'.

8 Examples are: Grocyn (1446–1519) in 1488–90; Linacre (1460–1524) in 1486–92; Colet (1467–1519) in 1493–96.

9 The phrase quoted is taken from Ridolfi's article on Machiavelli in the *Encyclopaedia Britannica,* 15th edition, Macropaedia v. 11, p. 230. See also Roberto Ridolfi, *Vita di Niccolò Machiavelli,* 2 vols (4th edn. 1969); English translation by Cecil Grayson (London 1963).

10 Machiavelli's *Discourses on Livy,* Book II, ch. 12. English translation by Leslie J. Walker S.J., 2 vols, 1950; paperback edition, edited by Bernard Crick, Harmondsworth 1970.

11 See Frances Yates, *The Rosicrucian Enlightenment* (London 1972), and Peter French's study of the Elizabethan Magus, *John Dee* (London 1972). In her earlier book, *Giordano Bruno and the Hermetic Tradition* (London 1964), Frances Yates traced the tradition from its formation in Renaissance Italy by Marsilio Ficino and Pico della Mirandola, and continued her study of it in Renaissance England in *Theatre of the World* (London 1969).

12 Paul Oskar Kristeller, *Renaissance Thought and its Sources,* ed. by Michael Mooney (New York 1979), pp. 167–68. See also, in the same collection of essays, Number 4 on 'Paganism and Christianity' and Number 9 on 'The Dignity of Man'.

13 Among the earliest of these manuals was Francisco Patrizi's *The Kingdom and the Education of the King* from the 1470s, and among northern examples Erasmus's *The Education of a Christian Prince,* completed in 1519 and presented to Francis II. They were supplemented by an equally necessary series, of which Castiglione's *The Courtier,* based on his experiences at the court of Urbino, provided the prototype. An English example is Sir Thomas Elyot's *The Book Named the Governor* (1531), and a Spanish example, Guevara's *The Dial of Princes,* said to have been the most widely read book in sixteenth-century Europe after the Bible.

14 André Chastel. 'The Arts during the Renaissance' in *The Renaissance: Essays in Interpretation* (London 1982), p. 238. The quotation from Raphael's letter to Leo X is taken from the same essay.

Chapter II The Enlightenment

1 Peter Gay, *The Enlightenment*, v. I, *The Rise of Modern Paganism* (London 1970), p. 3.

2 Francis Bacon, *Novum Organon*, Aphorism 84. A convenient translation, which I have used, is published in a collection of texts edited by Edwin A. Burtt, *The English Philosophers, From Bacon to Mill* (New York 1939), p. 58.

3 The preface to the *Novum Organon*, Burtt, *op. cit.*, p. 25.

4 Gay, *op. cit.*, v. I, pp. 269–279.

5 Voltaire, *Examen important de Milord Bolingbroke*, in *Oeuvres complètes*, ed. Louis Moland, v. XXVI, p. 198.

6 Diderot, (25 September 1762), *Correspondance*, ed. Georges Roth, v. IV, p. 178.

7 Voltaire, *Sermon des cinquante*, published in 1762 but written ten years before at the Prussian court. *Oeuvres complètes*, v. XXIV, pp. 354–55.

8 Diderot, *Oeuvres philosophiques*, ed. P. Vernière (Paris 1956), pp. 240–41.

9 *Ibid.*, p. 191.

10 Two famous examples are the Lunar Society of Birmingham, of which James Watt, Matthew Boulton and Joseph Priestley were members; and Benjamin Franklin's American Philosophical Society, founded in Philadelphia in 1743.

11 Montesquieu, *Considérations sur les causes de la grandeur et de la décadence des romains* (1734), *Oeuvres complètes*, Nagel ed., 3 vols, v. I (Paris 1950), p. 482. Robert Shackleton has shown that the passage quoted was directly inspired by a passage in *La vita civile* by Vico's friend, the little-known Neapolitan philosopher, Paolo Mattia Doria. See Robert Shackleton, *Montesquieu* (Oxford 1961), p. 168.

12 *Hume's Treatise*, ed. L. A. Selby-Bigge (Oxford 1888), p. xx.

13 Condillac, *Essai sur l'origine des connaissances humaines*, in *Oeuvres philosophiques*, ed. Georges Le Roy, 3 vols (1947–51), v. I, p. 4.

14 *Hume's Treatise*, p. 13.

15 Quoted by Norman Hampson, *The Enlightenment* (Harmondsworth 1968), pp. 122–23.

16 A. J. Ayer, *Hume* (Oxford 1980), p. 96.

17 Descartes, *Les passions de l'âme*, 1649, Art. 50 (ed. G. Rodis Lewis, Paris 1955).

18 Hume, *An Enquiry concerning Human Understanding*, p. 25 of L. A. Selby-Bigge (ed.), *Enquiries concerning Human Understanding and Concerning the Principles of Morals*, by David Hume, 3rd. ed. rev. by P. H. Nidditch (Oxford 1975).

19 *Hume's Treatise*, p. 415.

20 Diderot, *Pensées philosophiques*, in *Oeuvres complètes*, ed. J. Assézat and M. Tourneux, 20 vols (1875–77), v. I, p. 127.

21 *Hume's Treatise*, p. 487.

22 Hume, *Enquiry*, p. 75.

23 *Hume's Treatise*, p. 183

24 Including the fact that Rousseau was for a time a popular composer and widely known for his writings on music, a subject on which he wrote all the entries in the *Encylopédie*. Gay, *op. cit.*, v. II, pp. 534–35.

25 Rousseau, *Oeuvres complètes*, Pléiade edition, ed. by B. Gagnebin, M. Raymond *et. al.*, 4 vols (Paris 1959), v. I, p. 7.

26 *Ibid.*, p. 351.

27 Rousseau, *Dialogue troisième, Rousseau juge de Jean-Jacques*, ibid., p. 936.

28 Rousseau, *Oeuvres* (Paris 1964), v. III, p. 164.

29 Rousseau on himself in *Dialogue Troisieme, Oeuvres*, v. I, pp. 934–35.

30 Rousseau, *Emile ou de l'education*, edition Garnier Frères (Paris 1964), p. 76.

31 *Ibid.*, pp. 103–04.

32 *Dialogue Troisieme, Oeuvres*, v. I, pp. 934–35.

33 David Hume, 'Of the Standard of Taste', *Philosophical Works*, ed. T. H. Green and T. H. Grose, 4 vols (1882), v. III, p. 271.

34 Nikolaus Pevsner, *An Outline of European Architecture*, Jubilee edition (London 1960), pp. 624–25.

35 These were delivered between 1769 and 1790. See Sir Joshua Reynolds, *Discourses on Art*, ed. Robert R. Wark, 2nd edn. (New Haven 1975).

36 Sir Isaiah Berlin, *Vico and Herder* (London 1976), p. 147. Herder's own *Ideen zur Philosophie der Geschichte der Menschheit* (1784–91) (abridged transl. ed. by Frank E. Manuel, *Reflections on the Philosophy of the History of Mankind*, Chicago 1968) was left unfinished.

37 Quoted in Berlin, *op. cit.*, p. 165.

38 *Ibid.*, p. 158.

39 Kant, *Critique of Pure Reason*, Engl. transl. by Norman Kemp Smith (London 1933), p. 65.

40 Kant, *Fundamental Principles of the Metaphysics of Morals*, Engl. transl. by T. K. Abbott in *Kant's Critique of Practical Reason and other works on the Theory of Ethics*, 5th ed. (London 1898), p. 18.

41 Kant, *Critique of Judgment*, Engl. transl. by J. H. Bernard (New York 1951), p. 37.

42 That enthusiastic radical, the Rev. Dr Richard Price, against whom Burke directed his celebrated *Reflections on the French Revolution*, declared that as 'a step in the progressive course of human improvement' the American Revolution ranked 'next to the introduction of Christianity among mankind'; and Tom Paine, in *Common Sense*, offered a vision of America which millions were to accept in the following century as an 'asylum for the persecuted lovers of civil and religious liberty from every part of Europe'.

43 Jean Joseph Mounier, *Recherches sur les courses qui ont empêché les Français de devenir libres, et sur les moyens qui leur restent pour acquérir la liberté*, 2 vols (Geneva 1792).

44 Mallet du Pan, *Correspondance politique pour servir à l'histoire du Républicanisme français* (Geneva 1796).

Chapter III   The Nineteenth Century: Rival Versions

1 Alexis de Tocqueville, *Journeys to England and Ireland*, Engl. transl. by G. Lawrence and K. P. Mayer, ed. by J. P. Mayer (London 1958), pp. 107–08.

2 Alexis de Tocqueville, *Oeuvres complètes*, 9 vols, 2nd edn. ed. by Gustave de Beaumont (Paris 1860–66), v. III, p. 514.

3 *Ibid.*, pp. 519–20.

4 *Ibid.*, v. V, pp. 425 *et seq.*

5 de Tocqueville to Henry Reeves, 22 March 1837; *ibid.*, v. VI, pp. 67–68.

6 *L'ancien régime et la revolution* was published in 1856; Engl. transl. by Stuart Gilbert (New York 1955).

7 de Tocqueville, *Oeuvres*, v. VIII, pp. 321–22.

8 Preface to *A Contribution to the Critique of Political Economy* (1859), Engl. transl. in T. B. Bottomore (ed.), *Karl Marx: Selected Writings in Sociology and Social Philosophy* (Harmondsworth 1970), pp. 51–52.

9 Sir Isaiah Berlin, *Karl Marx*, 4th ed. (Oxford 1978), p. 116.

10 Quoted in Barker Fairley, *A Study of Goethe* (Oxford 1947), p. 163.

11 *Ibidem.*

12 Quoted in W. H. Bruford, *The German Tradition of Self-Cultivation: 'Bildung' from Humboldt to Thomas Mann* (Cambridge 1973), p. 69.

13 *Ibid.*, p. 72.

14 *Ibid.*, p. 70.

15 Karl Barth, *Die protestantische Theologie im 19. Jahrhundert* (Zurich 1947), p. 379.

16 Wordsworth's sonnet was first published in 1807.

17 Mill's essay on Bentham was followed by a companion piece on Coleridge, also published in the *Westminster Review*, in 1840. They have been reprinted by the Cambridge University Press, with an introduction by F. R. Leavis, *Mill on Bentham and Coleridge* (1980). Mill's remarks on Bentham are to be found in the first essay, pp. 40 and 73.

18 Mill's remarks on Coleridge are to be found in the second essay, *ibid.*, pp. 108, 130, 132.

19 Thomas Carlyle, *Signs of the Times* (1829), in *Collected Works*, v. II, p. 233.

20 S. T. Coleridge, *Lay Sermons*, ed. R. J. White (London 1972), p. 205.

21 J. S. Mill, *Autobiography*, ed. H. J. Laski (Oxford 1924), p. 56.

22 Quoted by Michael St. John Packe from a letter of April 1834, in *The Life of John Stuart Mill* (London 1954), p 83.

23 Mill, *Autobiography*, p. 180.

24 Packe, *op. cit.*, p. 400.

25 Well summarized by Packe, *ibid.*, p. 402.

26 J. S. Mill, *On Liberty*, ed. R. B. McCallum (Oxford 1946), p. 104.

27 Mill, *Autobiography*, p. 216.

28 Quoted in Basil Willey, *Nineteenth Century Studies* (London 1949), p. 230.

29 *George Eliot's Life, as related in her letters and journals*, ed. J. W. Cross, 3 vols (Edinburgh 1885), v. III, p. 245.

30 Dated 5 July. Cross, *op. cit.*, v. II, p. 118.

31 In the introduction to *The Portable Matthew Arnold*, which he edited for the Viking Press (New York 1949), pp. 3–4.

32 Stanzas from 'The Grande Chartreuse', *ibid.*, p. 151.

33 *Ibid.*, p. 473.

34 *Ibid.*, pp. 476–79.

35 R. L. (later Sir Robert) Morant was the official at the Board of Education who drew up the act of 1902 abolishing the school board system and making county and county borough councils responsible for both elementary and secondary education in England and Wales. The Nonconformists strongly opposed the act, which was carried through by a Conservative government under A. J. Balfour.

36 Quoted in Basil Willey, *op. cit.*, p. 261.

37 John Ruskin, *The Stones of Venice*, v. II, ch. 6, 'The Nature of Gothic', pp. 163–65 of the 1899 edition.

38 William Morris, 'How I became a Socialist', reprinted in the Nonesuch Morris, ed. G. D. H. Cole (1948), pp. 657–58.

39 'Communism', *ibid.*, p. 663.

40 *The Wealth of Nations* (1778); J. S. Mill's *Principles of Political Economy* (1848); Alfred Marshall's *Principles of Economics*, 2nd edn. (1890).

41 *The Grammar of Science* (1892), p. 24.

42 Quoted by Michael Biddiss, *The Age of the Masses* (Harmondsworth 1977), p. 52.

43 See above, p. 106.

Chapter IV
The Twentieth Century:
Towards a New Humanism

1 No doubt we were only rediscovering for ourselves, as every generation has to do, what was obvious to our parents, but a lecture on 'When did the twentieth century begin?' which I gave in London in the early 1960s had sufficient novelty for a non-specialist audience to lead *The Times* to devote a leading article to it, and for the BBC to make it the introductory talk in a series on 'The Radical Years, 1900–14'. Its final appearance is in the Pelican Guides to

Modern Literature, as 'The Double Image' in the volume on *Modernism 1890–1930*, edited by Malcolm Bradbury and James McFarlane and first published in 1976. Other historians and critics, of course, were making the same discovery at much the same time.

2   Virginia Woolf, 'Mr Bennett and Mr Brown' (1924), reprinted in *Collected Essays* (London 1966), v. I. p. 321.

3   26 May 1898, quoted in Michael Meyer, *Henrik Ibsen*, v. 3. *The Top of the Cold Mountain, 1883–1906*, p. 297.

4   Nietzsche, *Werke*, 3 vols (2nd edn. Munich 1960), v. 2, *Die Fröhliche Wissenschaft*, p. 127.

5   Strindberg's Preface to *Miss Julie*, in *International Modern Plays* (Everyman Edn., London 1950), pp. 5–16.

6   Meyer, *op. cit.*, v. 3, p. 253.

7   John Fletcher and James McFarlane, 'Modernist Drama: Origins and Patterns', in *Modernism 1890–1930*, p. 504.

8   'The Name and Nature of Modernism', in *Modernism 1890–1930*, pp. 46–52.

9   For an account of the new radicalism in Britain before and after the First World War, see Peter Clarke, *Liberals and Social Democrats* (Cambridge 1978).

10   Finished 1905, published in 1922, and translated into English as *The Protestant Ethic and the Spirit of Capitalism* (London 1930).

11   Quoted by William James in *The Principles of Psychology*, v. I (New York 1904), p. 131.

12   Jacques Barzun (in *A Stroll with William James*, Chicago 1983) quotes Bergson's remark in a letter to James: 'People picture pragmatism *a priori* as something that must necessarily be simple . . . I ceaselessly repeat, on the contrary, that [it] is one of the most subtle and *nuancées* doctrines that has ever appeared in philosophy.' (p. 107). As an example of James's style, here is his description of the 'tender-minded' as opposed to the 'tough-minded' temperament (exactly the op-

posite of common usage today): The tender-minded wears 'a doctrinaire and authoritative complexion. The phrase "must be" is ever on its lips. The belly band of its universe must be tight. It wants something unexposed to accident, eternal and unalterable. The mutable in experience must be founded on immutability.' As an example of his originality here is his definition of experience: 'My experience is what I agree to attend to.'

13   Quoted in Ernest Jones, *The Life and Work of Sigmund Freud*, 3 vols (London 1953–57), v. II, pp. 417–18.

14   Heinz Hartmann, *Psychoanalysis and Moral Values* (1960), p. 17, quoted by Peter Gay, *Freud, Jews and Other Germans: Masters and Victims in Modernist Culture* (New York 1978), p. 69.

15   *'Civilised' Sexual Morality and Modern Nervous Illness* (1908), also quoted by Gay, *op. cit.*, p. 67.

16   Gay, *ibid.*, p. 70.

17   B. A. Farrell in the *Fontana Dictionary of Modern Thought* published in the US as the *Harper Dictionary of Modern Thought*, ed. Alan Bullock and Oliver Stallybrass (1977), p. 247.

18   Revised 1947, and reprinted in *The Liberal Imagination* (New York 1950).

19   See Joseph Campbell, *The Hero with a Thousand Faces*, 2nd edn. (Princeton 1968).

20   John Menken, one of the members of the Baca seminar (see preface, p. 7) had worked as a young apprentice on Frank Lloyd Wright's famous house at Taliesin in New Mexico. He told us that Wright required every new apprentice to build and equip a carpenter's tool box: 'Almost as though woven into this task was the strong suggestion that he should familiarize himself with Emerson, Thoreau and Whitman'.

21   I recall two episodes with pleasure. One was the part I was able to play, as Chairman of the Trustees of the Tate Gallery, in securing Barbara Hepworth's house and garden (complete with sculptures) for the nation. The other was

working with the Danish architect, Arne Jacobsen, in the creation of St Catherine's College, Oxford, a modern college in an ancient university of which Sir Nikolaus Pevsner says: 'This is a perfect piece of architecture. It has a consistent plan and every detail is meticulously worked out. Self-discipline is its message, expressed in terms of a geometry pervading the whole and the parts, and felt wherever one moves or stops' (*The Buildings of England, Oxfordshire*, 1974). Both are illustrated in Plates XXV and XXVI.

22 Examples are *The Cabinet of Dr Caligari*; *Metropolis*; Chaplin's *City Lights* and *Modern Times*; Jean Renoir's *A Day in the Country* and *The Rules of the Game*; Eisenstein's *Battleship Potemkin*.

23 Kafka died in Vienna, virtually unknown, in 1924. *The Trial* was published posthumously in 1925; *The Castle* in 1926.

24 Erich Heller, *Kafka* (London 1974), p. 26.

25 Pirandello's two best known plays were published in 1921 (*Six Characters in Search of an Author*) and 1922 (*Enrico IV*).

26 Gay, *Freud, Jews and Other Germans*, p. 26.

27 Quoted in W. H. Bruford, *op. cit.*, p. 231.

28 *Ibid.*, p. 246.

29 *Bekenntniss zum Sozialismus*, quoted in Bruford, *op. cit.*, p. 254.

30 For an example, see Diderot's *Le Neveu de Rameau* published in 1762. This so impressed Goethe that he translated it into German. Freud was equally delighted with Diderot's anticipation of the Oedipus complex.

31 Quoted in Eberhard Busch, *Karl Barth, his life from letters and autobiographical texts* (transl. from the 2nd revised German edition, London 1976), pp. 119–20.

32 *Ibid.*, p. 166.

33 Reprinted in Bertrand Russell, *Mysticism and Logic* (Anchor paperback edn., New York 1957), pp. 47–48.

34 Reinhold Niebuhr, *The Nature and Destiny of Man*, paperback edition (New York 1964), v. I, p. 188.

35 Quoted by John C. Bennett in his article on Niebuhr in the *Encyclopaedia Britannica*, 15th ed. Macropaedia, p. 74. Niebuhr develops his views on the relationship between the Kingdom of God and the realm of history in his Gifford lectures, *op. cit.*, v. II, *Human Destiny*.

Chapter V
Has Humanism a Future?

1 George Steiner, *In Bluebeard's Castle* (New Haven 1971), p. 63.

2 Thomas Mann, 'Geist und Wesen der deutschen Republik', June 1923, quoted in Bruford, *op. cit.*, p. vii.

3 Osip Mandelstam's comparison of Stalin's Russia with Assyria and Egypt is to be found in chapter 54 of Nadezhda Mandelstam's *Hope Against Hope*, transl. by Max Hayward (New York 1970). The quotation which follows forms the last paragraph of the chapter, on p. 308 of the Penguin edn. (Harmondsworth 1975).

4 I owe this illustration to Romesh and Raj Thapar, publisher and editor of the Indian journal *Seminar*, who were members of the Aspen Institute seminar at Baca (see p. 7).

5 Martin Luther King's letter is reprinted in *Afro-American History: Primary Sources*, ed. Thomas R. Frazier (New York 1970), pp. 392–405.

6 In his *Antigones* (Oxford 1984), p. 124.

7 See the portrait of the young Keynes in Robert Skidelsky, *John Maynard Keynes*, v. I, *Hopes Betrayed, 1883–1920* (London 1983).

8 *Report of the Committee of Inquiry on Industrial Democracy*. Cmnd. (1977), 6706.

List and Sources of Illustrations

the quarrel between Voltaire and Rousseau. *Bibliothèque Nationale, Paris*
58 Monument to Rousseau by Barbier. Engraving. *Bibliothèque Nationale, Paris*
59 Barbara Krafft, Posthumous portrait of Mozart, 1819. *Gesellschaft der Musikfreunde, Vienna*
60 Jean Baptiste Siméon Chardin, *La Gouvernante*. *National Gallery of Canada, Ottawa*
61 Title-page of Winckelmann's *History of the Art of Antiquity* 1764.
62 The temple of Neptune at Paestum, engraved by G. P. M. Dumont. From *Les Ruines de Paestum 1769*.
63 The Pantheon, Paris. Photo *Giraudon*
64 Henry Fuseli, *The Artist Moved by the Grandeur of Antique Fragments*, 1778–9. *Kunsthaus, Zurich*
65 The American Declaration of Independence. *United States Information Service*
66 The Apotheosis of Rousseau. Engraving after Girardet, 1794. *British Museum, London*
67 Revolutionary wall poster. *Bibliothèque Nationale, Paris*
68 The Night of the 9–10 Thermidor, Year II. Musée Carnavalet, Paris. Photo *Giraudon*
69 Francisco Goya, *The Sleep of Reason Produces Monsters*. From *Caprichos, c. 1798*.
70 Ludovike Simanswiz, *Friedrich Schiller*, 1798. *Schiller-Nationalmuseum, Marbach*
71 Johann Stephen Decker, *Ludwig van Beethoven*, 1824. *Historisches Museum, Vienna*

72 Léon Noël, *Alexis de Tocqueville*. *Bibliothèque Nationale, Paris*
73 H. Edridge, *William Wordsworth*. Photo *BBC Hulton Picture Library*
74 Auguste Comte. Photo *BBC Hulton Picture Library*
75 F. W. Burton, *George Eliot*, 1865. *National Portrait Gallery, London*
76 Matthew Arnold. Photo *BBC Hulton Picture Library*
77 John Stuart Mill. Photo *BBC Hulton Picture Library*
78 William Morris. Hammersmith Central Library, London
79 A. F. Tait, *View of Stockport Viaduct*, 1848. *National Railway Museum, York*
80 French Declaration of the Rights of Man. *Bibliothèque Nationale, Paris*
81 The Great Exhibition at Crystal Palace, 1851. *British Library, London*
82 Propaganda print concerning the introduction of universal suffrage in France, 1851. *Bibliothèque Nationale, Paris*
83 Karl Marx. Photo *Mansell Collection*
84 View of Jena, *c.*1800. *British Library, London*
85 Drawing of the intermaxillary bone by Goethe. *Nationale Forschungs- und Gedenkstätten der klassischen deutschen Literatur, Weimar*
86 Sir Thomas Lawrence, *Wilhelm von Humboldt. Reproduced by gracious permission of Her Majesty the Queen*
87 The University of Berlin. From *Berlin und seine Umgebungen im neunzehnten Jahrhundert, 1833*.

88 Joseph Severn, *Shelley at the Baths of Caracalla Writing Prometheus Unbound*, 1845. *Keats-Shelley Memorial House, Rome*
89 The Krupps works at Essen, 1861. Photo *Krupp*
90 Brook Street ragged and industrial school. From *The Illustrated London News, 1853*.
91 Von Pech, *Henrik Ibsen*. Photo *Mansell Collection*
92 Sigmund Freud. Photo *The Bettmann Archive*
93 C. G. Jung. Photo *Campbell Studios*
94 Igor Stravinsky. Photo *Douglas Glass*
95 Thomas Mann. *Archiv der Akademie der Künste der Deutschen Demokratischen Republik, Berlin*
96 Max Weber, *Österreichische Nationalbibliothek, Vienna*
97 Albert Einstein. Photo *Associated Press*
98 Pablo Picasso. Photo *Lee Miller*
99 Bertrand Russell. Photo *Harold White*
100 Friedrich Nietzsche. Photo *BBC Hulton Picture Library*
101 Christian Krohg, *August Strindberg*, 1893. *Norsk Folkemuseum, Oslo*
102 Henry and William James. *Lamb House, Rye*
103 Taliesin West by Frank Lloyd Wright. Photo *Pedro Guerrero*
104 The Modulor, from Le Corbusier's *Le Modulor 1946*.
105 A scene from Fritz Lang's *Metropolis*, 1925–6. Photo *National Film Archive, London*
106 A scene from Charlie Chaplin's *Modern Times*, 1936. Metro Goldwyn Mayer/United Artists Entertainment Co. Photo

National Film Archive, London
107 & 108 Albert Schweitzer in Lambaréné, Africa, Photo *Erica Anderson*
109 Juan Genovés, *El Foco*, 1966. *Staatsgalerie, Stuttgart*
110 Nazi Party rally at Nuremberg, 1934. *National Archives, Washington*
111 German soldiers hoisting the Nazi war flag on the Acropolis. Photo *G. Sweeting*
112 Aerial view of Hanover, 1945. Photo *United States Air Force*
113 The gates of the Gdansk shipyard in Poland, August 1980. Photo *Solidarity with Solidarity*
114 The execution of a member of the French resistance during the German occupation. Photo *Roger-Viollet*
115 Mahatma Gandhi. Photo *Mansell Collection*
116 Demonstration of the mothers of the 'Plaza de Mayo' in Buenos Aires, 1983. Photo *Amnesty International*
117 A demonstration in London by members of the WSPU in June 1910. From *The Daily Sketch*, 20 June 1910
118 Martin Luther King addressing a meeting in Washington D.C., 28 August 1963. From Martin Luther King's *Why We Can't Wait* 1964.
119 Gwen Raverat, *John Maynard Keynes, c.*1908. *National Portrait Gallery, London*
120 Joseph Wright of Derby, *Arkwright's Cotton Mill, Cromford,. Private Collection*
121 The Ford Body Plant at Dagenham. Photo *Ford Motor Company*

Index

Italic numbers refer to the black and white illustrations and their captions; Roman numerals refer to the colour plates.

207